Seven Women: Great Painters

Winthrop & Frances Neilson

CHILTON BOOK COMPANY · *Philadelphia   New York   London*

A Bird flies high
A Bird flies far
A Bird flies near
Always fly, little Bird,
*   without fear.*

TO KALEEN
this book is dedicated

Acknowledgments

THE AUTHORS of this book wish to acknowledge the cooperation of a number of people and institutions for facilities used in the research on personalities in art who lived over a period of some two hundred years; for permission to use published material; and, for assistance in assembling the reproductions of works of the seven artists included here. To each one we express our grateful thanks, specifically:

To Mr. William W. Morrison, Assistant to the Director of the National Gallery of Art, Washington, D.C.; to Mr. Bartlett H. Hayes, Jr., Director, Addison Gallery of American Art, Andover, Massachusetts; to Mr. Otto Wittmann, Director, Toledo Museum of Art, Toledo, Ohio; and to the Wally F. Galleries in New York, for their special assistance in response to our requests for reproductions.

To Miss Ethel Ashton and Miss Louise Wallman of the Pennsylvania Academy of the Fine Arts, Philadelphia, Pennsylvania, for help, respectively, with the library files and archives of the Academy.

To Mr. Frederick A. Sweet, Curator of American Painting and Sculpture, the Art Institute of Chicago, and to his publisher, the University of Oklahoma Press, for permission to use in research his book, *Miss Mary Cassatt: Impressionist from Pennsylvania.*

To Dr. Evan Turner, Director of the Philadelphia Museum of Art, for his comments quoted in this book.

To the family of Cecilia Beaux for cooperation, especially Mrs. Henry Saltonstall for use of a treasured photograph, Mrs. Catherine Drinker Bowen, and Mrs. Frederic L. Ballard.

To Mr. Willis Harrison for use of his personal library.

And to Mr. and Mrs. Paul Mellon, and Mr. Andre Meyer; to the Museum of Modern Art, New York, the Philadelphia Museum of Art, the Brooklyn Museum, the Cleveland Museum of Art, the National Academy of Design, the National Collection of Fine Arts, The Smithsonian Institution, The Metropolitan Museum of Art, the Pennsylvania Academy of the Fine Arts, the National Gallery of Art, the Wally F. Galleries, the Royal Academy of Arts in London, and the Gallery of the Uffizi in Florence, all for their kind permissions to reproduce works from their collections in this book.

Contents

Plates

Seven Women:
Great Painters

CHAPTER 1

Seven Women

WOMEN ARTISTS? Painters? Perhaps, says the usual sceptic, but scarcely *great* painters. The sceptic may remember two or three, but, he adds, can they be considered really great?

The usual person finds difficulty in naming more than several women painters, historically. The doubtful ones will say that women and great art do not mix. Yet for generations women have been drawing, painting, and sculpturing. Numbers of them have been serious professionals. Why have not more survived the test of time?

In contemporary art the pattern has changed to some extent. A number of women are painting now who seem to have as reasonable a chance of achieving a lasting reputation as their male counterparts. The girl studying art today surely has a better opportunity for success than her grandmother had.

Even so, the proportion of successful female artists is remarkably low in relation to men. Questions do remain: are women constitutionally handicapped in such a way that they are, usually, doomed to failure in the fine arts? Are young girl students at so much a competitive disadvantage that they are predestined to the necessity of overcoming greater obstacles than the boys with whom they study? Is art actually a man's career?

This book provides an emphatic *no* as answer. The stories of those women who have achieved acknowledged and permanent recognition in the long story of art disprove any doubts about

1

the ability of the feminine sex to match the male in creative ability. In some ways, a woman's special intuition may give her advantages.

Then why have so few women attained greatness? This is a provocative question indeed.

At the moment thousands of girls are filling the art schools and the art departments of universities, probably more girls than men. Many of these students are specializing in the fine arts of painting and sculpture, excluding commercial fields and education. Are they wasting their time through years of intensive study and dreams because of unknown pitfalls? What about those women who have achieved contemporary success and whose work is shown in New York galleries and finds wall space in museums? Will they last, or due to some unforeseen prejudice will they fall into limbo sooner than male artists? The art collector is concerned, too. Should he pay less for a painting created by a woman than one done by a man, granted that present reputation and quality are equal?

This book hopefully answers the questions which do exist, regardless of sceptics and doubters, or those who on the other side believe in the absolute equality of the sexes. The seven women included in these pages have beyond question a permanency of reputation in art history. Their life stories, their contributions to the continuing stream of art, and their specific skills and knowledge reach far past the borders of the times in which they lived.

Each one of these women was entirely different in personality from the others. Several had similarities of family background, despite nationality differences, but their educations, academically as well as in art, were strikingly unalike. Their lifetime experiences regardless of their times had little in common. Superficially at least, these seven were as divergent and as individual as any seven artists, male or female, could be expected to be.

It is curious, however, to search for some common denominators between all seven. Slowly, in studying their lives and work, one does find factors in common, certain things which had major bearing on their ultimate success. These factors in their relationships to each begin to answer the questions about the careers of women generally in the fine arts.

Of the seven women who are subjects of this book, three are

American (Cassatt, Beaux, O'Keeffe), three are French (Vigée-Lebrun, Morisot, Laurencin), one was Swiss (Kauffmann). Two spent most of their lives as expatriates from their own countries (Kauffmann and Cassatt). All of them traveled considerably, either by choice or necessity. The three Frenchwomen, all of whom grew up in or near Paris, were the ones to remain closest to the places of their birth.

Five of these painters were married, one twice (Kauff-mann). Two had unhappy marriages (Kauffmann and Lauren-cin), including twice-married Angelica Kauffmann whose first union was a fraud. Two married ones had children, one daughter each (Vigée-Lebrun and Morisot). Relations of these mothers with their children were completely happy.

The painting output of the seven came somewhat closer to similarity. Two were distinctly portrait painters with little other work (Vigée-Lebrun and Beaux). Another was primarily a por-traitist, although she became known even more for other sub-jects, although these did contain figures (Kauffmann). Two others also painted portraits, but were mainly concerned with painting for its own sake, so that portraits became a part of their whole direction (Morisot and Cassatt). The sixth was fa-mous for idealistic figures, some close to true portraiture (Lau-rencin), while the last did not use human figures at all (Georgia O'Keeffe).

In painting style, only one accepted the "status quo" of her day, not attempting to break tradition (Cecilia Beaux). One other took advantage of a new trend, and went along with it, helping its development (Kauffmann). A third rebelled in a quiet way against prevailing custom, and naively helped a re-turn to simple basics (Vigée-Lebrun). Two others were dis-tinctly radicals in their work, joining with extremists of their time (Morisot and Cassatt). Still one more began her career with radicals, but then developed an absolutely distinct style of her own (Marie Laurencin). So did the final painter, but she was an individualist all the way from school days (O'Keeffe).

Of the seven, two received first instruction from their fathers, painters themselves but of far lesser rank than their daughters (Kauffmann, Vigée-Lebrun). Of the other five, every one in more or less degree began with banal or conservative instruc-tion which they unanimously rejected. Five were deeply influ-enced by the study and copying of works of great masters in

3

museums. All seven, with the possible exception of one (O'Keeffe) depended greatly on the advice and help of older, experienced male painters.

Two of the painters achieved reputations in their teens (Kauffmann, Vigée-Lebrun). One never began art study in earnest until she was twenty (Laurencin). All the others became serious professionals in their early twenties, after certain self-doubt.

From these statistics, it is hard to find a common denominator, or any guide of help to contemporary girls seriously dedicating themselves to art.

Yet further study of these seven lives reveals fascinating points of similarity. All these women came from families of reasonable financial resources, or they became independent at an early age through their work. Only one, in the latter category, had childhood money difficulties (Vigée-Lebrun). None, through their lifetime careers, had real security problems, even though progress was not always as easy as they would have wished. Every one sold paintings, some with great success, others more slowly.

Every one appeared to have an instinctive skill in drawing and a quick perception in color and composition, which instruction readily brought to remarkable fruition. Once the final decision by each woman was made to dedicate herself to painting, she expended every bit of herself on work, work and more work. Even the ones with family responsibilities continued to work. It is difficult to define the word "genius," and as a term it is better forgotten. What these girls had, as girls, was a natural instinct, plus guidance, and then utmost interest and effort in their work.

If "genius" is some kind of excuse for believing that anyone can be a master without great effort, none of these women had it. Parenthetically, no one has ever had it, man or woman, in art or anything else.

One specific point in common among these seven women was self-confidence in themselves, once they made up their minds to undertake the hard road of art. There was never over-confidence, but they were all sure of their goals even while searching for new ways, and they never wavered in their own individuality of expression. They did not follow fashions or trends for the sake of popularity. They expressed what they believed in, disregarding risks of popular disapproval.

These points of similarity between seven great women artists can be the first guidelines for contemporaries to judge themselves and be judged by others. They are standards for serious students who hope to achieve success, whether girls or boys.

Yet beyond skill and intuition and work, more than external factors or luck, more than all else, a more important bond linked these seven women. Without it, they would still have failed and now be only a memory. This most important, all important, common denominator is personality.

In this interpretation, personality is stimulation, or outgiving to others, or ease in being with people. It means attracting the friends who matter to one's own individuality. Perhaps some men can skulk in dark corners, produce a masterpiece and have it acknowledged. It appears that a woman cannot, if the records correctly tell the stories. Herein does lie one inequality.

Angelica Kauffmann had personality which made her welcome among the loftiest circles of Italian and English society, from whom she drew her clients, as well as popular with the public which approved her. Elisabeth Vigée-Lebrun had the poise and presence to portray royalty and become the "painter of Queens." Berthe Morisot could hold a social position as a focal point of Impressionism in Paris as well as being a painter as qualified as most of that famous group. Mary Cassatt had the experience and keenness to win over to her the French, a foreigner in their land. Cecilia Beaux could tactfully do portraits of great men of history, and Marie Laurencin had a particular charm which made her a favorite of all Paris. And our Georgia O'Keeffe's strength of purpose and character influenced her friends in New York for many years, and her personality still affects the art culture of all America.

These women knew how to get along with people, how to be accepted. Here seems to be the clue to the true secret of the success of women artists, and the sad reason for the failure of lacklustre ones despite their own technical merit.

How does a woman develop for herself the poise that makes her an asset in the highest circles of the artistic and literary world, acceptable to the social and political elite? Personality is a natural attribute in the first place, but useless without cultivation of intelligence, manners, and ease. Beauty is not necessary, but magnetism is.

If the standard of magnetic personality is applied to each of the seven great women painters of the following pages, the ratings of every one reach the topmost bracket.

A disgruntled woman who lacks magnetism but who has the skill and creative ability to produce great works of art may rightly question the justice of this premise. Categorically, the answer must be that justice does not necessarily prevail in the art world. Furthermore, personal magnetism cannot help but carry over into produced works of art, giving the final touch that lifts them up into masterpieces which live on their own. There is such a subtle difference between skilled but routine art, and the glow of life which permeates the great.

Unfortunately for women, a man may more readily get away with lesser magnetism of his own personality, letting his work speak for him. At least, in studying the lives of great painters of all time, male and female, this presumption seems to be true.

It has been said that, between men and women artists, there is a basic personality difference which accounts for the few successful women in painting. The idea is that the female is directed by temperament toward creativity in child-bearing and care, the creation of home and family, whereas the male drive is toward work and fulfillment in a career. Perhaps this to a degree is true. The world may have lost many great artists to the basic urge to create children rather than pictures. Yet historically there is little to support this theory as an absolute fact. What of the success of women in other forms of art, especially in literature?

Women have borne children and also created great works in literature, music and drama, dance, and in the fine arts as well. Beyond the boundaries of art there are the female achievements in creative science. So the theory must be reduced to proper proportions.

To select just seven women who have achieved lasting greatness as painters is a matter of difficult judgment. Some readers may disapprove of exclusions, and, indeed, inclusions, but fortunately criticism in art is traditional, and must stand on its own merit as well as the work criticized. For example, it may be asked why the omission of Rosa Bonheur, one of the most popular women painters. Reproductions of her animal paintings have been favorites with children for many years, especially of her "Horse Fair," now in New York's Metropolitan Museum of Art.

Rosa Bonheur was born in Bordeaux, France, in 1822. She had unquestioned skill in drawing, as her smooth renditions of animals attest. She, too, had a strong and vibrant personality. Shortly before she died in 1899 she was given the Grand Cross of the French Legion of Honor, the first woman so rewarded. However, Rosa Bonheur seemed more an illustrator than one who achieved greatness in the fine arts tradition of the seven included here.

Moreover, of the contemporary women painting today, surely some will reach lasting greatness. Time, not this book, must dictate their futures.

Art, by its nature, is a substance of personal opinion. May it always be so!

PLATE 1

Self-portrait, by Angelica Kauffmann.
*The Pennsylvania Academy
of the Fine Arts, Philadelphia.*

CHAPTER 2

Angelica Kauffmann

1741–1807

OR CENTURIES, art history was barren of women painters. The classical eras, the Middle Ages and the flowering Renaissance were in the hands of men. If gentle ladies doodled, or if others may have been serious enough to earn a little money by producing pictures, their names have gone. As far as any reputation or record endures, the role of the female in art was limited to models, or subjects of portraits.

Then, in the middle 1750s, a young Swiss girl made her startling debut. Like a blazing meteor crashing into the ranks of males, Angelica Kauffmann set a merry pace for other women to follow. Her life reads like a novel, and, in fact, novels have been based on her story.[11,12] She rose to fame even in childhood, but she was artist enough never to allow her work to slip below her own standards throughout all her long life.

Angelica Kauffmann was born in 1741 in the Swiss village of Coir, in the District of Chur.[1] Her father made a precarious living as a portrait painter, and her family was poor. Angelica's early life was unsettled, as her father moved from place to place in search of new business. Ultimately, changing surroundings helped Angelica as she had greater opportunities to visit museums, and finally, to study and copy masterwork paintings.

Things were different in those days. Maria Anna Angelica, her full name, did not have schooling as she would now. Her father, the portraitist, taught her how to make paintings from

9

the time when she was very young. At nine years of age she could help him earn money. By the time she was twelve, she not only could do portraits on her own but she had a particular gift for music, too. She became an unexpected celebrity in Switzerland, a child prodigy whose work the rich and influential came to see and to hear her sing as well.[14]

Her mother and father, undoubtedly anticipating danger in their daughter's unprecedented success, decided there must be a respite. Willingly or not, Angelica was shipped off for a prolonged visit to her uncle who was a goatherd in the remote hills of Switzerland.[9] Living in primitive conditions, far from an inquisitive and admiring public, she gained a discernment of values and a wariness of false adulation. The goatherd's wisdom, which came from leading a contemplative life, must have been passed to the child in long discussions. Angelica learned to be careful, an ability which failed her only once in a lifetime filled with dizzying events and friendships.

Back with her traveling family, Angelica had constant opportunity to see and learn from the art in museums everywhere. Her ambition grew. Once her father took her to Milan, her first trip to Italy. Then, when Angelica was fifteen, the Kauffmann family went to Rome.[9]

In Rome, her career really started. She was developing into a girl of a special kind of beauty with large, dark eyes and sensitive mouth. At this particular stage of history, beauty was a feminine quality especially appreciated. Angelica left a long record of herself through a series of self-portraits. Certainly her success in society justified what she portrayed of herself in paint. (See Plate 1, an undated self-portrait but undoubtedly done when she was young.)

Her increasing talents matched her growing beauty and charm. Angelica at this time of her life was faced with a major decision: should she continue with painting, or turn to a career in opera? Apparently she was equally talented for either choice. She seemed to have realized that she could not do both. Painting must be as equally demanding in its vigorous training as the constant practice a singer must undergo. She selected fine arts, and painted a nostalgic allegorical picture of a girl being lured by Music on one hand and Painting on the other.[9]

At fifteen the Italians took Angelica Kauffmann to their hearts with great enthusiasm. She was the "child prodigy" again, tal-

ented, beautiful and able to speak four languages. Then her
mother died. The illusion of youth in a lovely dream burst
apart. Her father received a commission to do paintings for a
church in Switzerland. She returned to help him with this work.

Afterward, on her own, she went back to Rome,[9] a city where
she knew she would grow in ability and knowledge. Rome, one
vast museum in its own right, offered her everything.

ANGELICA KAUFFMANN's life coincided with another of the changes
in the story of art which has always marked its progress. The
clarity of the Renaissance, the "rebirth" of Art out of the
medieval times, with its beginning from Giotto to its ending
with the latter life of Michelangelo, had given way to the
Baroque. Baroque art and architecture, with ornate decoration
and flamboyancy, had in turn deteriorated into the Rococo.
This style of ornament and art developed in France during
the reign of Louis XV (early and mid-1750s), and was used to
extremes in other parts of Europe. Its character was, in architecture and decoration, gilt scrollwork and forms in inverse designs, and shells of various patterns. In painting the subjects
were sentimental and gaudy. As a revolt of public opinion and
taste, the fine arts of painting and sculpture, and architecture,
too, were turning back to the ancient classics, represented by
Greek and early Italian themes, in a style that was "neo-classic." This compounded classic themes with styles as they had
been used over three hundred years before, in the early Renaissance. It was not a "rebirth," really, in that sense of the
word, but rather a "new classic" art based on ancient origins.
By "classic," it must be understood that the term meant then
greater realism, more effective simplicity not only in subject matter but in technique.

To divert into generalities for a moment, the story of Art has
always been an effort to move forward, to try new ideas and
new methods. But the very effort of a new line of approach has
often bogged down into a falsity of endeavor, as, one might say,
one puts another layer of icing on the cake over the first, and
then still another, until the cake, which was good in the first
place, becomes soggy and collapses under the weight of the layers. Then public taste, with bad indigestion, says, "What was
the matter with the original cake? Let's go back to just that,
and start over again." This has happened a number of times

in art, particularly in ancient Greek and Roman sculpture when the Romans superimposed their ideas on the simplicity, and knowledge, of the Greeks and found themselves with heavy, massive pieces of sculpture during the time of the Empire which could never match the naturalness of the early Greeks.

It happened unintentionally when Early Christian painting began in Rome, and the painters of that time had lost all knowledge of perspective and form which had been discovered centuries before in earlier civilizations. They had to begin the art of painting over again, with naive simplicity. The results were beautiful because of their lack of "sophistication." Then that primitive quality became lost in the Middle Ages until the Renaissance discovered its beauty and brought it out anew with techniques of its own.

So, at the beginning of Angelica Kauffmann's painting career, the public was tired of the multiple layers of Baroque icing on the cake. They wanted the cake itself, the original of which was hanging on palace walls, in churches, and in the historic landmarks all over Italy. It was a kind of "Renaissance" in its way, where the people demanded what used to be good.

To divert still further and look at Art History at the immediate time of writing this book, it is very difficult to bake a new cake that is the same that Grandma used to make. The materials are different. The taste of food is different.

Perhaps, and only perhaps, for who can say at the moment of ferment, in this latter part of the twentieth century we have added so many layers on top of the cake that we cannot find the original, and it would be stale by now if we did. Yet the layers themselves, because of the fantastic mixtures we have put so fast one on top of another, have become inedible. We ourselves have to dump out the mess we have made, and start a new cake. But it must be our own, to our own taste, not what someone did many years ago.

This was not, in the light of history, what Angelica Kauffmann did. Artists then went back to the past, and revived it. They did it well, and the public was pleased for a long time, nearly a hundred years. After Angelica's era, the revival sank again into sentimentality and inertia until broken by the boldness of the Impressionists.

Angelica did not know what would happen, and she could

have done nothing about it if she had. Which one of us today knows where Art is going, and what we could do if we did?

In any case, the demand in Art was toward a revival of the classical Italian. It spread over Rome, and through Italy. Angelica saw what was wanted, studied it, and used it. In doing so, she found a place for herself in the forefront of painting.

She went to Florence, and somehow obtained permission from the authorities to go into the Uffizi and Pitti Palaces and copy paintings. Women were not welcome to do such a thing as this. It was most unusual, and she may have been the first to be given the privilege. It is said that male students working there resented her presence among them, notwithstanding her beautiful eyes for which she was noted.[9]

Then in Rome, Angelica met Johann Joachim Winckelmann, a German archaeologist and art historian. He had become renowned even at a young age (he died at fifty-one) for his studies of Greek and Roman antiquities. He had the knowledge that Angelica wanted. From him she learned of mythology, and the meanings of religious and allegorical art. Rome was an endless source of study. This knowledge made it possible for Angelica to fall into the new tide of art swinging toward the classical.

She learned, and she painted, and her reputation grew. At this moment, England was in turmoil, tired of Rococo, anxious for anything from Italy. The gentlemen of England went to Italy to finish their educations, and returned filled with the glory of ancient Rome and beauty of the Renaissance. England turned to Italy. The best painters responded.

It is not surprising that Angelica Kauffmann responded, too. She did so at the urging of Lady Wentworth, the wife of the British Ambassador. Under her auspices Angelica moved to London. The year was 1766, and Angelica was twenty-five.[9]

SHE hit London like a storm, with the fullness of her Swiss-Latin beauty. A painter with an established reputation, she had the charm which earned her a place anywhere. Angelica moved immediately into the highest social ranks strata, and was a special favorite at the English royal court. Celebrities flocked to her for portraits.

Her style of painting especially, a neo-classic or pseudo-classic Italian manner, was just what the English wanted.

One of her first portraits was of David Garrick, the celebrated English actor. Then she met Sir Joshua Reynolds, the gruff Englishman who was, and is, considered one of the leading painters, especially of portraits, of his era.

For the first time, as clearly as the records show, love came into Angelica Kauffmann's life. Sir Joshua was in his early forties when he met Angelica. He was a bachelor, and wanted nothing else for himself. But the two began an affair, which, the story of Angelica indicates, may have gone on for many years. He did two portraits of Angelica, and she did one of him. He helped and advised her, although at the beginning perhaps she needed little advice. He was painting in his own individual manner. The new wave of neo-classicism was not to his inclination or interest. He went on with his own interpretations. He recognized Angelica's ability, however, and did help her to obtain painting commissions.[14]

At that time the popular designers of furniture and interiors were the Adam brothers. There were four of them of whom Robert was the most celebrated. The name itself has become a dictionary word for a certain type of design, especially furniture, fireplace mantels, and wall and ceiling panels. These were mostly designs with straight lines embellished with painting medallions and scenes of Italian classic origin. Robert had known of Angelica in Rome, and he, too, had urged her to go to England.[9]

The designing work of the Adams needed painting to fill out the white plaster barrenness of empty spaces. She became best known at that time for her work in supplementing the Adam designs. Her knowledge of Greek and Roman mythology came to the fore.

Angelica was not only popular in English social circles, but she was very busy. She was like a star in the British court social functions (in the time of King George III, before the American Revolution). Angelica did portraits of the hierarchy of the group; she knew the painters in London, Gainsborough among them; and she had countless proposals of marriage.

She was in love with Sir Joshua, but she had to forget the idea of marriage with him. He was too much of a bachelor. At that time she made the mistake of her life, perhaps the only one she ever made. A Swedish count arrived in London, Frederick de Horn, who smoothly and easily swept her off her feet.

She accepted his offer of marriage. All was well until suddenly the real Count de Horn appeared and exposed Angelica's husband as his own former valet. The story goes that the interloper had already married and left a girl in Germany.[9]

The blow to Angelica was terrible. It was more perhaps a matter of pride than love. The English government arranged a settlement on the valet, whose real name was Brandt, on condition that he get out of England at once. He did, taking much of Angelica's money with him.

Angelica continued her work but avoided social affairs in London from that time on. Sir Joshua Reynolds was still her friend, and now she did need his help. She continued painting portraits and doing the work commissioned by the Adam brothers. Actually, Sir Joshua himself was responsible for her doing a good deal of this decorative work, as he asked Angelica to do his own fireplace mantel at the beginning.

The English people went on to enjoy Angelica's neo-classic subjects. She had a further intuition about this. Middle-class Englishmen were going through an aspect of prudery about nudes in art, always a basic subject of painting and sculpture. Angelica met their possible objections by a discreet handling of draperies in such a way that sensibilities were not affected. Her popularity rose among the middle class as much as it existed among upper groups in the social scale.[9]

Her time of trouble was assuaged by her friends who stood by her. King George III himself came to have his portrait painted. Angelica's popularity remained high. No one blamed her for the perfidy of the Swede. Nevertheless, her marriage was a blight on her life for years. Why a marriage contract to a bigamist was not annulled seems curious. Perhaps the decision was hers. In any case, she felt bound until the day of her "husband's" death.

Meantime, among the leading English artists, her name appeared on a petition to the king for the establishment of a Royal Academy of Arts. Sir Joshua may have been instrumental in having her included.

The grant requested by the petitioners for an Academy was given by the king. The Royal Academy was founded, and Angelica Kauffmann is listed as one of the founders.[14] In the catalogue of the first show, in 1769 (only three years after her arrival in England), her exhibit was followed by the initials,

15

"R.A.," which has since become one of the most distinguished honors earned by English painters. Granted that the word "academic" has come to mean traditional, conservative, "stuffy," and is looked down upon by modern painters as an objectionable term, and that its meaning stems from the Royal Academy, from the French Academy, and from the National Academy in New York, still these institutions inside their "stuffy" walls do preserve valued records which would otherwise be lost. Everything seems to have its place.

Another woman, one Mary Moser, also signed the Royal Academy petition.[9] She must have been a painter. She seems to be forgotten otherwise. The trail of artists once known and then forgotten is something like the long lines of drying buffalo skulls along the paths of the West. It is a terrible prospect for artists to face. Difficult enough is the fearful job of making a reputation during one's lifetime. To be forgotten later, irrevocably, and never to know it, has to be an artist's nightmare.

Angelica Kauffmann lives, and the number of paintings she left with the Royal Academy helps prove it. She did ceiling designs for the vestibule of the Academy. (Plates 2, 3, 4, and 5.) One of the major commissions of her life was to do part of the decorations in St. Paul's Church in London. She shared this work with Sir Joshua Reynolds, Cipriani, the Italian who had come to London at the same time she did, and Benjamin West, the American expatriate painter who spent most of his life in England. West painted the famous portrait of Benjamin Franklin on the latter's English visit before the Revolution.

Angelica left in England many records of her work. She became a landmark in English art history, although she was not English at all. Her false Swedish husband lived on almost fourteen years. When he died she was truly free, though she might have made the point from the beginning that marriage to an already married man was illegal and void.

Once free, she did marry again. This time her husband was an artist, an Italian who had also come to London. Antonio Zucchi was a painter from Venice. He, too, had done a number of designs and medallions for the Adam brothers. Angelica and Antonio spoke the same language, figuratively and literally. Both were artists of the same style and ideas.

By the time Angelica was able to marry, she was forty. The older Zucchi did not achieve her fame; she was far better in her work. Yet they were completely compatible in their life together. The marriage worked wonderfully.

Angelica and her new husband promptly left England for Italy. They settled in Rome and became a part of the gay and bright social life of that vibrant city. Angelica received commission after commission for paintings, and once again she was a favorite in the exalted circles of titled families.

Rome has been for centuries an international gathering place for artists, writers, musicians, historians, poets by all means, those deeply involved or perhaps only on the fringes of the arts. Rome is something of a roost for these people from all over the world, and contains a large international settlement to which additions come and subtractions drift away. The city has always been this way, more uniquely so than Paris or modern New York, except that sometimes troublesome wars interfere with the pleasant sharing of Italian life.

Another foreigner still growing in reputation who came to Rome was Johann Wolfgang Goethe, who was then only destined to achieve one of the greatest reputations in world literature. Angelica met Goethe, eight years younger than she was, and they became immediate friends. Goethe was unmarried, inclined to romance, especially in Italy. The story goes that he was recovering from one affair when he met Angelica, beautiful with dark eyes, charming manner and personality, intelligent as an artist who for years had moved among the nobility. Goethe must have had romantic ideas immediately. Angelica, according to the record, refused. She was happily married. All the entreaties which we can surmise a strong-willed Goethe must have made did not prevail on her. Their friendship remained merely just that, although it was a close and warm one,[9] and in all likelihood included Angelica's husband as well.

Goethe dedicated his novel, *Egmont,* to Angelica, and she in turn designed the frontispiece for the first edition.

In Rome Angelica's reputation and popularity continued to grow. Commissions came increasingly. She still rode the wave that had carried her so far. Angelica continued to be a star that glowed steadily and brightly.

Those years in Rome were prosperous and happy, until in 1795 Angelica's husband died.[9] She was then fifty-four. The death of Zucchi came at about the time of Napoleon's rise to power in France, and the invasion of Italy. Rome was in a ferment.

a part of that era which was so highly social, flamboyant, and rich in the nobility. The years in which she lived marked the peak of royal elegance. King George III of England paid her the tribute of sitting for his portrait at the same moment he was having difficulties with the troublesome revolutionaries establishing independence in America. The French Revolution tore this kind of world apart, but Napoleon Bonaparte built it back again in conquered Italy. Angelica went through personal and financial difficulties in a Europe of violent change, but she survived it all without tarnish to her reputation or a break in her friendships. This was much due to her own character and good sense. She was Swiss, the daughter of a poor painter, and perhaps she did remember the wisdom of her uncle, the goatherd in the lonely hills. Certainly she kept a personal balance in a society known for its giddiness and intrigue.

Yet that was not all. Angelica Kauffmann did have a solid lifetime hold on an ability to paint that was no mere youthful show of genius. She worked hard for all that she received. She understood what she was doing, and she never underestimated the challenge of art or the lessons she could gain from earlier masters.

Art has been in a continuing flow of change. One phase has always followed another, as true now in our day as it was before. The difference is only in time.

Some centuries intervened between the greatest glory of ancient Greece to the height of Imperial Rome with its fabulous architectural arches. Christian primitive painting in Rome carried on for several hundred years. Between Giotto and Raphael there were two hundred years. Michelangelo, near the end of the Renaissance, lived to be far older than Raphael. The Baroque that followed with Borromini and Bernini, with their fanciful decorations, still covered a long period. The more modern French Impressionism lasted about forty years, fading into Neo- and Post-Impressionism, then Cubism and the various other art "isms." Finally, the emphatic art cycle of the New York School of Abstract Expressionism, the "drip school" with its variations, lasted ten years. Pop art was worth two or three years, op not much more than one. At this moment conflicting phases of art may not last even one season.

If art seems to change unreasonably fast over its history, so furiously fast now compared to Angelica Kauffmann's time,

then it is wise to stop for a moment and look at other things:
the sciences and medicine. Exactly the same things have happened in those fields. Da Vinci may have drawn an airplane
on paper, but how long intervened before the Wright brothers
made one fly?

Those who are remembered especially in the arts, and in the
sciences, are those in the forefront of change. Angelica Kauffmann caught the same tide at a time of popular revulsion
against a post-Baroque drift into overstuffed sentimentality. The
current on which she rode was in a sense a backward one: a
feeling of wishing to return to classic Greek, Roman, and early
Renaissance styles and themes. Because things moved slowly then,
she had time to carry through for her lifetime the ideas that
were in demand.

When times changed again, the paintings of Angelica Kauffmann seemed outdated, as they now do to many. They appear sentimental, or overdone, or the portraits themselves dark.
They should not be so considered.

Angelica Kauffmann's paintings are as closely tied to history
as anything else that transpired in her time. As achievements
they are outstanding. If she cannot measure up to the most famous of her day, well, do we say it was because she was a
woman? That would not be fair or true.

There must have been other women who were professional
painters, too. Actually, there were. But they did not leave their
works in St. Paul's Cathedral, their portrait work in museums
all over Europe, their record in London's Royal Academy. Angelica Kauffmann did.

ANGELICA's self-portrait reproduced (Plate 1) was clearly done
when she was a young woman. It is not dated, so that only
surmise can guess her age.

Records indicate that the picture was given to Dr. John Morgan of Philadelphia for services rendered in Rome.[16] What the
services were, or why an American doctor would have helped
the young Swiss painter in Italy, is not clear. And perhaps the
doctor asked for a portrait in lieu of a monetary fee, for there
is no evidence to suggest that Angelica in her early years in
Rome was financially pressed. We can deduce, however, that
Dr. Morgan came into possession of the painting while Angelica
was living in Rome during her early twenties. Our surmise,

AN ANALYSIS
OF THE
REPRODUCED
PAINTINGS

therefore, can place her age when she did the self-portrait at somewhere between twenty and twenty-five.

The painting came into possession of the Pennsylvania Academy of the Fine Arts in Philadelphia in 1811, when it was first exhibited there. The Academy began its existence in 1805, and Angelica's self-portrait is among the earliest of the treasures in its collection.

Portraits in that day, as indeed a good many conservative ones still are, were made with dark, almost black backgrounds. Into the backgrounds the heads, figures and costuming were meticulously worked. Angelica's portrayal of herself, one of many she did, followed the established manner. She used a dark background, but out of it glows a young, gently modeled portrait.

Angelica shows her skill in drawing and her knowledge of form in this early painting. One can feel the roundness of the head, and the softness of the hair as it turns back and away. The line of the hair over the forehead and down the side of the cheek is obscured, keeping the head as a whole and not divided. The features are softly and beautifully drawn. So are the earring and the lace collar.

The composition of the portrait appears deceptively simple. The head itself is placed in exactly the right position, slightly to the left. The midline of the picture is approximately at the bridge of the nose. Notice how the lace collar, even though drawn in detail, follows the roundness of form and complements the face rather than pulling one's eye from the features. The half circle of the tiara, more suggested than drawn, offsets the opposite half circle of the collar. Then the further half circle where the arm is rounded off beneath the shoulder becomes a basically important part of the whole composition, bringing the portrait into an entirety. Visualize, if you can, the arm being carried to the bottom edge instead of rounded off. The whole picture could lose its character.

In the portrait's drawing and composition, attention is inevitably focused again and again to the eyes, Angelica's most distinguishing feature. As a portrait, the result is remarkably effective and pleasing. This skill was to earn for Angelica the commissions to do portraits of George III, the nobility, and the most famous personages of England and continental Europe.

The four other reproductions of Angelica's paintings are from ceiling murals which she painted for the Royal Academy of

Arts, Piccadilly, London. (Plates 2, 3, 4, and 5.) The four represent an entirely different approach and creative feeling than her portraits. All are indicative of Angelica Kauffmann's background, as well as of the neo-classic demands then in style. As a Swiss girl, she remembered the snow-capped mountains. As one familiar with the antiquities of Rome, she knew the sacred columns and the old sculpture. As a painter, she put new life into subjects that might have come from worn-out ideas after the Renaissance. Yet all are done with her own personal skill in drawing and in composition, the kind of skill that bridges any difference between men and women, and makes them equally fine artists.

The first one (Plate 2), of a girl deep in thought with her elbow resting on a carved marble base, shows again Angelica's outstanding ability in drawing. The figure of the girl, although fully clothed, is followed in form through the light tunic of the dress and the heavy folds of the mantle across her lap and legs. Her features and limbs are idealized. She is beautiful, in the classic manner. Yet her contemplation is in far-away intellectual realms. Beside her elbow is a set of chessmen with a game apparently in progress as a number of the pieces have been moved from the original starting point. Is she playing against an unseen adversary not in the picture? Probably not. In her right hand she holds a scientist's compass, and on a bench by her knee rests paper and pen, as if she had been writing.

This painting is not realistic. It preceded the era of Realism in art where everyone was in natural or commonplace surroundings. The figure of the girl is allegorical, representing "Genius," or merely a composition. There is no specific explanation for an idealized girl to be sitting at the chess game, out of doors, resting an elbow on the marble base of an antique column. The mountain and trees of the background are pure Italian Renaissance in style. Why should she be holding a scientific instrument and appear to be thinking between sentences? None of these apparent discrepancies matter in the least. The painting was done for the sake of its own decorative quality and its skillful execution.

The necessity for absolute explanation of the content of a work of art came later, and in our contemporary world has faded out again. As in Angelica Kauffmann's time and before her, art is created for the sake of its own impact, not to explain why

PLATE 2

24

PLATE 3

Composition, by Angelica Kauffmann.
Royal Academy of Arts, London.

25

PLATE 4

Design, by Angelica Kauffmann.
Royal Academy of Arts, London.

Composition, by Angelica Kauffmann.
Royal Academy of Arts, London.

27

within itself. Style now is very different, in the new non-realistic manner, but the intent is the same as in Angelica's ideals of beautiful painting.

These comments follow through where the other works reproduced from the Royal Academy ceilings are concerned. Another composition shows a different idealized female figure holding palette and paint brushes out of doors amid rocks and trees (Plate 5). The background shows a great range of mountains. A girl would not realistically be painting in that setting, dressed in long flowing gown, with one breast bare. The rainbow behind makes no more sense than the girl's strangely uplifted arm.

Discounting all the reasons for being "real," we are left with a beautifully designed composition, in the then-prevalent style of painting. Once again the motif is circular, with the rainbow arc balancing the long opposite curve of the girl's body. It is decorative, and if we no longer like the theme and say it is sentimental and old-fashioned we cannot deny that the essential compositional elements of opposing lines and forms, of "horizontals" and "verticals," are seen in recent abstractions in exactly the same way.

Art is simply a statement of old concepts in new ways, as long as the art work itself is "good." To know what is currently "good" is always difficult. Angelica Kauffmann would paint differently if she lived today. What she did had the quality to stand the test of time.

Her third painting reproduced (Plate 4) is called "Design." It is of another girl earnestly engaged in making a drawing from an ancient piece of sculpture. The antiquity is enhanced by the two Greek columns behind. The subject of this painting seems more understandable. It is what it is. But her dress seems fashioned after a Greek tunic. The picture is an excellent example of the "neo-classic."

Angelica Kauffmann's sense of the circular composition is clearly shown again, as the half circle of the girl's body leaning forward in work meets the arch of the bent piece of sculpture. This nearly perfect circle has the counter lines of the two vertical columns. The scrap of paper lying on the floor gives the underscoring completion to the whole composition. Even the way that piece of paper curls up at the end keeps the composition in place. These elements of any painting come from knowledge. They are never accidental.

As the first woman to achieve lasting fame in the long story of art, Angelica Kauffmann deserves our greatest respect. She knew the technique of painting as well as any man of her time, and she was able to use it to meet the demands of her public. Indeed, she has left a memorable body of work for generations that follow to appreciate.

PLATE 6

Self-portrait, by Elisabeth Louise Vigée-Lebrun.
Courtesy of Uffizi Gallery, Florence.

CHAPTER 3

Elisabeth Louise Vigée-Lebrun

1755–1842

ARIS was the birthplace of yet another girl destined for fame as a painter. Marie Anne Elisabeth Vigée was born on April 16, 1755, just fourteen years after the birth of Angelica Kauffmann. She was called by the diminutive "Lisette."

LISETTE

The careers of the two women had certain affinities. Lisette's father was also a portrait painter, although definitely of second-rate reputation. She, too, grew up in the atmosphere of art, with the smell of paint and turpentine from her father's studio pervading the house.

Lisette was sent to school in a convent from the time she was five until she was eleven.[19] It is pleasant to relate that her talent was supposed to have shown itself first at this age, for she was scolded by the sisters of the convent for drawing pictures in her books and on the walls. What child has not?

Her father did encourage her, and allowed her to draw and paint as she pleased. He did criticize the results, and gave her basic instruction in the techniques of art. There was a strong family attachment between Lisette and her father and mother, and when Lisette's father died suddenly when she was thirteen[19] it was a tragedy for her. He left his family with difficult financial problems, and a bleak outlook ahead.

Lisette by this time had the painting urge in earnest. Her mother sacrificed all she could, and entered Lisette in a studio run by one Gabriel Briard in the then-unfinished Louvre. Bri-

31

ard appears to have been another of those art teachers who have taken in beginning students and put them through academic procedures inept enough to discourage any youthful ambitions. When Lisette was told to start off by making a charcoal drawing of a plaster cast head, she was most unhappy. What life was there in a reproduction of a piece of sculpture that in itself was a step removed from life? With her father she had been drawing direct.[21]

But her mother had made a major effort to spare the money to send her to the school. To scorn it would have been ungrateful. So Lisette bore the tedium through the winter, and had to admit that her drawing improved. She was allowed to start painting, which she had done already with her father. Unlike her father, however, who had done it all for her, the instructor made her stretch and prepare her own canvas for painting. She had to accept a necessary discipline.

During that time a woman client of her father's came back to see if Lisette could finish a portrait left incomplete at the time of his death. Lisette refused to carry on what her father had started. She offered to make a new portrait at half the price. The woman accepted, and was so pleased with the result and the price that she sent friends to the youthful painter. They were all older women, insistent in their demands that they should be painted in the unnatural fashion of dress and jewelry then in vogue. Lisette was appalled by the falsity of it.[21]

She made a close friend at the studio school, a girl who lived in her neighborhood, and she asked her to pose for a portrait as Lisette herself wanted to do it. She used her friend's natural hair, and dressed her simply in a gown with a sash around her waist. What she painted was a portrait of naturalness, fresh, and unlike the heavy and ornate current styles.

A friend of her mother's saw the painting and immediately took it to a dealer. The dealer bought it, and displayed it in his window.

The details of this story are difficult to repeat with exact authority. The result does not need questioning. A French painter of great reputation, a favorite of the king, passed by the window and caught sight of Lisette's portrait. He was Joseph Vernet, the first of three generations of well-known artists in France, the son following the father, and grandson following the son. Vernet found out that the artist was the daughter of the Vigée whom he had known. He bought the picture, and immediately called on Lisette.

For the first time Lisette Vigée was receiving real acknowledgment. For a girl then about sixteen, this was a staggering honor.

Vernet looked at her other work, and gave her his soundest advice. Be careful of academic teaching, he said; he was afraid of it. He warned her of following any school or style of painting. She should study nature and the old masters, the ones who had proven themselves truly great. This was exactly what Lisette wanted to hear.[19]

Lisette Vigée had been born at a time when the glory of France was at its zenith, but decaying underneath. The powerful Louis XIV had been succeeded some time before by Louis XV, far weaker and less able to control his kingdom. The colonies in Canada were lost to the British during his reign. The French economy was shaky, although no one wanted to admit it. The nobility of France had established themselves with great wealth and power. Noble families were by right exempt from taxation and the burden of government expense fell on the common people who were kept in a state of poverty. Affluent and profligate, the nobility ruled the land, and, with ease and luxury constantly at hand, fell with time into a decadent society.

Decadence naturally affected fashions, manners, customs, and art. This historical background was a major influence on the career of Elisabeth Louise Vigée. Popular painters conformed to public taste with sentimentality, overdone compositions, sweetness. They used color, but the value of it was lost. Fragonard, one of the best, tried to rebel, but his famous painting of the little girl in the swing was about as far as he could go, and it is still crushed with sentimentality. Jean-Baptiste Greuze, equally or better known, did rebel, and his work achieved a greater sincerity and simplicity. Joseph Vernet understood, but did little. He was too popular with the nobility to risk it.

Against the prevailing mood, young Lisette bloomed suddenly like a fresh flower. Vernet invited her to his house and introduced her to his friends. They saw the simple portrait in Vernet's salon. They responded instantly. Titled ladies wanted her to do their portraits. They came in their carriages to Lisette's modest home to pose in her studio, the one used by her unsuccessful father. Sometimes there were two or three in a day. She

33

was overwhelmed with commissions, and had those with the most exalted titles waiting their turn.²¹ She was guided by Vernet's advice, where price was concerned, that a figure that seemed too high made the painting more appreciated.

Lisette had grown beautiful, with long brown curls and the natural glow of youth. She had charming manners and a sparkling personality. She became a favorite of society, and was invited to the great dinners and supper parties of the titled aristocracy. Social activities became so time-consuming that she had to refuse all dinner invitations because they infringed on her afternoon work. She restricted herself to suppers where the elite of Paris congregated.

Then the first of two important events happened to the young Lisette. At twenty-one she married. Jean Baptiste Lebrun had appeared in her life.¹⁹ He was pleasant, handsome, kind (which he always remained), and apparently did well financially. He had an art gallery where he bought and sold paintings, not contemporary ones but old masters. The pictures in his gallery were impressive for their value and the reputation of the artists who painted them. Lisette's mother had been remarried after her husband's death to a jeweler with an avaricious temperament. Lisette's stepfather as a matter of routine took the earnings from her painting for household expenses. He had been a source of difficulty for Lisette for a long time, trying to influence her work always toward greater profits. Lisette longed to escape. When Jean Lebrun proposed marriage, she was glad to accept. After all, everything about him was promising, and an attentive husband also interested in art could not have been a happier prospect.

After their marriage, she added her husband's name to her own to become Madame Vigée-Lebrun. She quickly discovered that she had exchanged a small financial leech for a larger one. Her stepfather had taken her money to pay household expenses. Her husband let her work for him, and he took her money for everything including his own gambling debts. The art gallery that appeared prosperous was a farce. Most of the paintings in it were on consignment or had been bought on credit which Jean Lebrun could not carry through. His wife's portrait earnings went toward his obligations. Yet Lisette accepted the situation. She had little choice. They seemed to have been happily married.

Meanwhile, King Louis XV of France had died, and been succeeded by Louis XVI, who loved hunting far more than his responsibilities. Marie Antoinette became queen, and the court of Versailles was more brilliant than ever with social functions, frivolities, intrigues, and a great outpouring of money. The families of the nobility spent their time, and financial wealth, in maintaining and increasing their prestige and favoritism in endless competition. Fashion was the way of life.

Lisette attended one dinner party given by the Duchesse de Magarin when the hostess made an attempt to outdo all other parties in sensation. Sixty guests were seated at the table, and the servants carried in an enormous pie. It was set before the assemblage, and the top removed. Out from the pie flew a hundred small live birds, twittering and chirping. The surprise turned to disaster. The frightened birds scattered in every direction, beyond control. Many of them settled on the heads of hysterical ladies, and their feet became entangled with the ornately arranged, piled-up hair, then so fashionable. Costumes were ruined, and to the chagrin of the duchesse, her party was a fiasco.

Louis XVI became king in 1774 at a momentous time in history. Soon ominous news came across the ocean from America. *Liberty, equality . . . taxation without representation is tyranny* . . . the words fell on the ears of the common people of France who suffered in poverty and worked beyond endurance to maintain their superiors, the aristocracy, and to pay the taxes needed to support the king's government. Those American words were like distant thunder announcing a coming storm. The nobility was too busy to hear, and the king was, too.

This story is part of history, but history was the backdrop for Elisabeth Vigée-Lebrun. She was caught up in the social whirl of Paris. It became a mark of prestige to be painted by the young woman artist who showed such original freshness in her work. To have her as a guest at social functions was a coup for the hostess. Lisette was pleased, happy, and intensely hard at work. Her commissions made possible her husband's acquisition of a new house, complete with servants, carriages and the necessary equipment to preserve social standing. He could spend more on gambling. Lisette herself shared in this kind of life naively, without understanding what it meant. All she tried to do through tact and persuasion was to have her sitters pose in simpler costumes than the outlandish hair ornaments and gowns that fashion required.

MARIE
ANTOINETTE

AT LAST the ultimate achievement came to Elisabeth Vigée-Lebrun. She received word that the queen wished her to come to Versailles. Marie Antoinette wanted to have her portrait done. It is not often that a portrait painter is commissioned by a head of state. Also, this was France and Lisette was a woman. Such an accolade was indeed news in Paris.

Lisette went to Versailles trembling, carrying her box of paints and empty canvas. She found the queen stiff and formal at first. But the two were exactly the same age. Lisette's charm and beauty, and above all her simplicity, were irresistible. It was not long before Marie Antoinette and Vigée-Lebrun were close friends, as close as a subject could be to Marie Antoinette, Queen of France.

The first commissioned portrait was followed by a number of others. Lisette became known as the painter of the queen of France, and her reputation grew throughout Europe. Before this she had given birth to a daughter, Julie. Motherhood was her other point in common with Marie Antoinette. There is a story that during one pregnancy (it must have ended in a miscarriage, for she did not speak of a second child), Lisette had pains and one day could not keep an appointment with the queen at Versailles. There was not time to send word. The queen was naturally annoyed. The next day she received Lisette to hear her explanation. Instantly Lisette was forgiven. In her confusion, a box full of paints and brushes spilled over the floor. Marie Antoinette herself stooped to pick them up. An expectant mother should not bend over so much, the queen said.[18]

In 1783 Elisabeth Vigée-Lebrun was invited to become a member of the French Academy. Her sponsor in submitting her name was her old friend, Joseph Vernet. Some difficulty arose in persuading the Academicians to admit a woman. They had several already, women whose names have been forgotten. Another story grew out of this, that only Marie Antoinette's intercession with the king made His Majesty order the Academy to accept Vigée-Lebrun. She herself emphatically denied the story, saying that it was a calumny against her. She was admitted on the basis of a painting which she did especially for the occasion. Its title was "Peace Bringing Back Abundance," a composition of two figures with a feeling of the classic.[18]

As an Academician, Elisabeth Vigée-Lebrun had the opportunities of showing without questioning in the annual Salon Exhibitions. In one of these shows, the usual candid expression of her art ran headlong into the French political difficulties that were approaching the breaking point.

In portraying Marie Antoinette on canvas, Lisette finally prevailed upon the queen to pose without the formal dress and appurtenances of royalty. She persuaded the sovereign queen of France to put on a simple white gown and straw hat. The picture which resulted was particularly successful as a portrait and as a painting. Vigée-Lebrun herself commented on her favorite subject when she said that the queen walked well, held her head erect, and had a clear, brilliant complexion.[18] In this painting, made after a trip with her husband to Belgium where she had an opportunity to study the colors of Rubens, Lisette exerted all her experience as an artist to approach the Flemish and Dutch classic schools in artistry. She could not, as she well knew, but neither could other French artists of that time.

Elisabeth Louise Vigée-Lebrun, as she has since become known in museums in Europe and America, was always an artist. It happened that portraits were her medium, her means of livelihood for her family and a rapacious husband. When she could finally convince the queen of France to pose in a costume that truly represented her own self-expression and interest, it was for the sake of art, not because her subject was a queen or that she would gain by that fact. Thinking of herself and of her contribution to art, the combination of what she wanted and of subject was so natural. Who else has ever had such an opportunity?

It did not work. Lisette, still young, lived in her own world of art. She had Paris at her feet, she was famous. She was not spoiled by the popularity of the world in which she moved. She was aloof from it, as any artist must be in the deep loneliness of the studio when no outside influence can intrude between the canvas and the painter. So Elisabeth Vigée-Lebrun conceived and carried out the portrait of her queen and friend, Marie Antoinette. The specific portrait likeness was done at the palace of Versailles. The personal touches that raise a painter into the realm of greatness were finished in the studio.

37

Marie Antoinette liked the painting and approved it. So did the king himself. So did everyone who saw it, from the standpoint of a great artistic achievement.

Yet Lisette, oblivious to current politics and the fast-growing storm approaching France, had no idea of the feelings of the people toward the queen. Knowing that she had a good painting, she put it into the annual exhibition of the Paris Salon. She had been warned by her friends, but she could not believe them. To be certain, she went to one of the opening days with her face hidden by a veil to listen to what the public said.

She was shocked, dismayed. No one objected to her style of painting. No one looked at it as a work of art at all. The public expressed their venomous feelings against the queen. To think that the queen of France would allow herself to be painted in a chemise! (The simple white dress.) And that she would wear a peasant's straw hat! Who did she think she was? These were among the comments. All the vituperation that had been building up over years against Marie Antoinette was poured out at the sight of a painting of her.[18]

This may have been the first time in the history of art that a painting became the pinpoint of popular disapproval for political reasons. It may still be the outstanding example to this day. Artists have been castigated for their espousal of social reforms and for many causes. But to have a painting in itself figuratively torn apart by the opposition of the "left" was, and is, unique.

With the distressed urging of Elisabeth Vigée-Lebrun, her treasured painting of Marie Antoinette was removed from the Paris Salon Exhibition the following day. The queen bore the brunt of the criticism for the informality of the portrait. Lisette took the blame to herself for persuading her queen to accept her idea.[18]

Finally the portrait painter of the queen and of the nobility had to face what her own simple comprehension had failed to see. After centuries of near-enslavement the common population of France was rising in revolt. Signs were evident everywhere: lack of respect from workmen on the street, insolent attitudes on the part of servants in her own home, clandestine meetings which her husband attended, the popularity of Benjamin Franklin, the wise American in Paris who worked for his struggling new country in the cause of freedom, and especially the new song that was being sung in the streets, *Marchons, marchons.* . . .

Her husband did not warn her. She was still making money from her work. She tried to shut her eyes to what was happening. Her friends left Paris. One by one the household servants dropped out. She was so badly treated on the street that she stopped appearing in public.

Elisabeth Vigée-Lebrun was a friend of the queen. She was marked. Marie Antoinette no longer sent for her. She, too, knew what friendship with the queen could mean.

STILL Lisette held on. She stopped painting. She had no heart to continue when it was dangerous even for her daughter to appear on the street. She was told to leave Paris, but she could not believe the reason given. What had she done? She was not of the nobility, she had hurt no one, she had merely worked for her living and tried to make her own contribution to the art of France.

The impulses of an enraged population have no reasoning. The mob is either for or against. In Paris the growing Revolution muttered under its breath for a long time. A vicious outbreak of people against people does not occur overnight. It takes years, or centuries, of oppression to bring out the bestial qualities of man. In Paris there was justification. All the same, the restless population did everything that could have been done by way of warning and protest. The king and the nobility would not, and did not, respond.

Once loose, the power of the mob sweeps over all, like the invading storm of the sea. Nothing, nothing, can wall it in or check its fury.

Still, Lisette could not understand. She did not until the enraged mobs of Paris stormed the invincible fortress of the Bastille and reduced it to a ruin. Then she realized. And one night a gang of ruffians invaded her own house and warned her that she must not flee. She must stay under surveillance.[21]

It was almost too late to try to escape. Her servants had left. Her carriage was marked. There was such an exodus from Paris that she could not get a reservation on the regular stagecoach.

On the very day on which King Louis XVI and Queen Marie Antoinette were brought by the civilian mob from Versailles into Paris, Elisabeth and her daughter escaped. It was October, 1789. They left on a coach traveling south, disguised as serving people in wooden shoes. The only reason they were able to make good

39

their escape was because the gates of Paris were carelessly left unguarded that night. The great march to Versailles and back to Paris had left the revolutionaries exhausted.[19]

She left Paris with only minutes to spare and achieved safety. Madame Vigée-Lebrun was already on the blacklist for execution by the guillotine. She could have joined the thousands of men, women and children whose necks were severed and whose blood poured in floods over the streets of Paris.

A painter serves the standards of art. An artist must stand free of politics in dedication to a basic expression of all humanity. It is not always possible. Lisette proved this fact. The subjects of her portraits, which still remain as living records of her time, are on museum walls. So many of the people themselves, her friends, her patrons, vanished in the maelstrom of the Revolution. Their heads, over which Lisette labored so carefully, disappeared in the bloody baskets under the guillotine.

Lisette made a hazardous journey to safety through France to the border of Italy. The whole French countryside was aroused. Even toward the end of her trip a fellow-traveler in the stage-coach, who had professed Revolutionary ideals, grinned at her and asked, "Where are your paint brushes, Madame Lebrun?" He was apparently escaping also, and his comments had been meant to throw off suspicion.[21]

She left her husband in Paris. All along, he had apparently ingratiated himself with the revolutionaries. Her brother remained, too, in safety. Only Lisette herself was listed for execution. She was the friend of the queen.

Once in Italy, Lisette found for herself how her reputation had traveled before her. She was accepted and honored everywhere. She went on to Rome and was at once flooded with portrait commissions.

But on the way to Rome she saw in Florence the self-portrait of Angelica Kauffmann who was then working in Rome. Lisette had the pleasure of meeting her, and spending two evenings in her company.[19] If the conversation between the first two women destined to be remembered as great painters in all the long history of art could have been recorded, it would be fascinating. Perhaps it was little more than any two in the same field meeting together, but this was hardly likely. Both by then were famous, both had painted royalty. Elisabeth, the younger one by fourteen years, respected Angelica. And Angelica knew what her younger colleague had achieved. Surely their meetings were interesting. Rome keeps its secrets.

Her own self-portrait is also in the Ufizzi (Plate 6).

While she was in Rome she received word that the Pope would be pleased to have her do his portrait. The stipulation, however, was made that she must come to the sitting veiled. To paint with her vision so obscured seemed an impossible condition, and she refused. She regretted having to do so, however, for reportedly she remarked that "Pius VI was one of the handsomest men that could be found." [19]

LISETTE was restless. She was too French to settle down in Rome, and too anxious about France. She moved on to Naples, where the queen of that Italian state was Marie Antoinette's sister. She painted that branch of the royal family. She went to Vienna, and again did a great number of portraits. Next was Russia, and on the morning when she had an appointment to start a portrait of Catherine the Great, the empress suddenly died. Still traveling, Lisette did a portrait of the queen of Prussia, and finally went to England.[21]

Everywhere her reputation preceded her. The fame of Elisabeth Vigée-Lebrun was spread far and wide. In England, George IV, then Prince of Wales, was a sitter for his portrait, and so was Lord Byron. As an artist she was received without question. Only the greatest skill could justify such a confidence.

At last she was free to return to her home in Paris. The rioting and the sound of the tumbril wheels on the way to the guillotine had ceased. Napoleon had taken over France, and restored order to a shaken country. Lisette, as her husband still must have called her, rejoined him after an absence of some twelve years. Jean Baptiste Lebrun died while still young. Julie, her daughter, had married a Russian and she, too, died. Elisabeth was left in Paris, her home, with many memories of those who had gone.

She continued her painting up to the time of her death at the age of eighty-seven, in Paris in 1842.

Few people, painters or not, have known so many historically important people. A fitting epitaph is the title already inscribed to her: "The Painter of Queens."

ELISABETH LOUISE VIGÉE-LEBRUN is known today as the second woman painter who has survived time which erases names with heartless cruelty. Why?

From the beginning she said of herself, "My passion for painting was born in me." [18] That passion gripped her through all
her lifetime, in spite of the troubles that would have pulled any
ordinary person from the track which she followed.

She had from her youngest days an extraordinary skill in drawing and in capturing likenesses in portraits. The ability to make
portraits comes from a natural perception, or sense of "seeing."
Without skill in drawing, this kind of perception would be
wasted.

What is skill in drawing? Some people have it with little instruction, while to others it can be acquired only by the longest
practice. It is nevertheless a "learned" skill available to almost
everyone willing to spend the time to learn. The ability to draw
comes, after long or short practice, like the sense of balance in
riding a bicycle. At first one falls, perhaps many times. Suddenly
there is the inner sense of balance, and then one can ride a
bicycle for the rest of his life without further conscious effort.

So it is with drawing. Yet, unlike bicycle riding, there are
degrees of drawing ability. The difference lies in "seeing," and
here perhaps it is innate or inherited capability which takes
over. How quickly, or to what degree, "seeing" can be learned
is a matter of argument.

Again what is "seeing"? In drawing, it is the power to translate
the model, or object, into one's own artistic expression. Individual
variations are just as wide as the number of people who draw.

Lisette Vigée-Lebrun had a special sense of drawing, or "seeing." Perhaps the sisters at her convent school had a legitimate
complaint after all in catching her at drawing on walls and in
books. This talent served her early in life, and never left her.

Still, the ability to see and draw the model is only a technical
skill. To become a great artist requires far more than technique.
Lisette's personality was probably the key to her success. She
could communicate her sincerity to her work. She hated the
pompous styles and manners of her time. She had the courage
to toss aside all that she could, reaching the heart of reality.
This brought out the freshness in her work which made her so
popular. Freshness and sincerity had been forgotten qualities in
French society.

Undeniably, Lisette's own charm and beauty helped her to
fame. She was an asset to have at parties. The sitters who posed
for her were captivated.

Early in her career, when those first women of the neighborhood began coming for their portraits, Lisette learned to please them. She made her portraits remarkable likenesses, as well as character studies. Yet she did take care to forget flaws and blemishes in her subjects: maybe some lines of age, or pock marks, or bloated jowls could be narrowed. She did not violate her honesty in portrayal. It was simply that if a person could see himself just a little closer to what he would like to be, rather than what he really was, he was more pleased.

Elisabeth Vigée-Lebrun did not establish new trends in art. She eliminated over-sentimentality from her painting, but did not set new styles, and probably was of little actual influence on other artists.

Her place in art history is perhaps most interesting for its external aspects. She did set a pace for women artists to follow. Women artists? Why make a differentiation? Elisabeth Vigée-Lebrun was essentially a woman, and as a painter used her feminine equalities in her work. Her portraits show a woman's sensitivity. Her life was distinctly her own as a daughter, wife and mother, besides her career as a successful professional.

So she proved that a woman could be an artist in her own feminine right, not trying to enter a man's world but remaining in her own. This is the final and conclusive reason why her name and works mean what they do today.

A SPECIAL QUALITY runs through the portraits by Elisabeth Vigée-Lebrun. It is a quality of life. Long before, and certainly long afterward, "portraits" were heavy and wooden. Other parts of this book refer to this characteristic. The dark, oppressive heaviness of portraiture nearly killed this form of fine art until our era. Vigée-Lebrun did not paint this way.

Remarkably, if the young Lisette were alive and painting today, she would still be enormously successful. She had a brightness, an aliveness, which has seldom existed in portraits. Each one, including her own self-portrait, catches the sitter in a normal, act-of-life pose. She had a contagious quality which belonged to her. Traditionally, portrait painters seem to inoculate themselves against life by their own self-imposed rules of trying to please their sitters and buyers. For several hundred years, painters of portraits—in general, it must be said, for certainly there were some exceptions—were merely commercial artists.

THE
PORTRAITS
REPRODUCED

Today it should be repeated, Elisabeth Vigée-Lebrun would have been known in Paris and the rest of Europe as she was in her own time, and her reputation would be equally great in New York. The President of the United States would never have rejected a portrait by Lisette.

The reproductions of her portraits here are best considered in a group. The naturalness carries through all of them. In looking at each reproduction in order (Plates 6, 7, and Color Plate 1), slowly and with time to absorb them, the first impact is that the artist was deriving pleasure in painting them. No one can doubt that to her painting was enjoyable, a full pleasure of living. Her subjects were pleased, too, even if one of them was herself (Plate 6). The second impact is how clearly her drawing justifies the reputation accredited to her.

This was Elisabeth Louise Vigée-Lebrun, Parisienne heart and soul, the painter of royalty . . . and people.

PLATE 7

Lady Folding a Letter, by Elisabeth Louise Vigée-Lebru
The Toledo Museum of Art,
gift of Edward Drummond Libbey.

Portrait of Berthe Morisot, by Edouard Manet.
The Cleveland Museum of Art,
Leonard C. Hanna Jr. Collection.

CHAPTER 4

Berthe Morisot

1841–1895

N PARIS, during the 1870's, events in the art world shocked the French capital and changed the history of art from that time until this very day. A group of dissatisfied French painters, mostly young, banded together in a revolt against the academicians who controlled contemporary taste and tradition. Their rebellion, fought against public opinion and through fearful financial difficulties, eventually opened up the whole field of modern art.

Remarkably, two young girls joined the band of radicals and, through the quality of their work, rose to the high ranks of famous artists. It was remarkable not only because both came from families of conservative and conventional backgrounds but, even more surprising, one girl was French and the other American— Berthe Morisot and Mary Cassatt.

The real revolution began in the year 1874 when this group of French painters put on a joint exhibition of their works with the common intention of shattering the tradition of dark, sentimental studio styles which had evolved in Europe from the colorful post-Renaissance, Baroque and neo-classic eras into a kind of art devoid of vitality and detached from reality of life. They sought again, and in a new way for color and subjects which would be a part of everyday living, for a technique that would take their work out of sombreness into vibrant meaning. The revolution was chiefly against the academic Salon, the annual Paris exhibition which controlled French art.

47

The show was held on the third floor of a photographer's studio on the Boulevard des Capucines in Paris.[5] The reaction was an explosion. Critics, newspapers and the public joined in a fury of disgust, ridicule and antipathy to the new form of art. These people professing themselves artists were labelled renegades, radicals, extremists. It is said that police had to be called out to prevent public riots of protest.

One of the group was Claude Monet, who showed a picture with the title, "Impression—Rising Sun." It was a painting of early morning across a river with a small boat in the foreground and shapes of ships and docks shrouded in blue mist through which a brilliant red sun cast rays across the rippling water surface. A disdainful newspaper critic picked up the title, and, intending to provoke public laughter, called the whole show "Impressionism." His readers did laugh, but the name stuck and the Impressionist movement was born.*

One of those in the exhibition was Berthe Morisot. Mary Cassatt appeared later.

Berthe Morisot (pronounced *Bert Morisōh*) was born in 1841 in Bourges, a city in central France. Her father was a high-ranking government official, holding then the title of Prefect of Bourges, an office somewhat equivalent to mayor of the town or district. Later, he was appointed to a government post in Paris, and moved his family there. Berthe, with two older sisters and a younger brother, grew up in the comfortable, secluded surroundings of a wealthy family. Schooling was conventional, in the usual manner for young ladies whose education was limited by the simple necessities of being future hostesses and wise mothers.[24] Lives were sheltered, and social functions carefully prescribed.

Whether or not at Berthe's own suggestion, when she was sixteen her mother decided that all three sisters should have painting lessons. Perhaps Berthe had an inherent longing, or perhaps her mother believed it was a nice idea. To be able to paint was a pleasant asset for a girl, like playing the piano or harp—not to be taken seriously. So the three Morisot children went to a local art teacher. One sister lost interest quickly. The other two did

---

* Another painting by Monet, "On the Terrace," in 1967, was bought at auction in London for a record-breaking $1,400,000, by the Metropolitan Museum of Art. The artist first received for it the sum of $41.

not like their teacher and wanted to change. Berthe and her sister, Edma, both began to feel the intensity that grips true artists.

They studied then with a man named Guichard who was in turn a follower of Delacroix, one of the very great French master painters and draftsmen. They stayed with Guichard for three years. Perhaps this teacher, who has otherwise faded into the shadows, made the contribution of his life by passing on to his young girl students the visions of what art truly meant.

Then, when Berthe was nineteen and Edma twenty, they sought out another teacher, a painter who made a specialty of working outdoors among fields and farms and forests glowing with sunlight. It must have been a choice of intuition, or because Berthe loved nature for itself. Most painters then remained in their studios using static subjects with dark, glossy backgrounds. The new teacher was Corot, a friend of Berthe's father who frequently visited the Morisot house.[8]

Jean Baptiste Camille Corot was sixty-four years old when young Berthe and Edma went to him. As a younger man he had spent much time in Italy, and found there the sunny skies and the joys of the natural outdoors. His painting turned in the direction of nature: landscapes, trees, hillsides glowing in mists from valleys. Sentimental, they might be called by today's harsh realists. Corot, with his love of nature, helped immeasurably to open the way to the Impressionists who closely followed him. There were others, too, besides Corot, who had the same ideals, in England as well as France, but Corot in a quiet, unassuming manner gained a major place in the story of French art of a hundred and more years ago.*

Corot helped Berthe Morisot find what she instinctively sought. He set her on her course. She did like the out of doors, and the sunshine, and the simple things of nature. She studied with him for six years,[24] and his imprint on her later work was definite. In a way, it was through her that part of his influence on the Impressionists was carried on to them.

All this time Edma continued to work with Berthe with equal enthusiasm. They were constantly together, and both of them reached professional stature by being accepted in the annual ex-

---

* Recently, at an auction in New York, a Corot painting brought a price of $310,000.

hibitions of the Paris Salon, whose judges and juries ruled who should be artists and who should not. Then Edma fell in love, and was married and had to move with her husband far from Paris. It meant a complete break with art. Edma wrote back letters of homesickness and frustration to Berthe expressing veiled regret at what she had done. Berthe's answer was reproving; she must remember how fortunate she was with her husband.

If Edma had continued her career, would the two Morisot girls have achieved equal rank? Would they have followed the same techniques? Their background influences and training were the same, uniquely so. What might have happened makes interesting speculation. It can be only speculation, for Berthe alone went on.[22]

One day Berthe was copying a painting in the Louvre for self-discipline and study, and while there she met a man who introduced himself as Edouard Manet. Certainly she knew of him. This was in 1868, and already Manet, at thirty-six, had rocked Paris with his two most scandalous paintings, "Luncheon on the Grass" and "Olympia." The first showed a nude girl sitting under trees with two fashionably dressed men, complete to neckties. One even wore a beret, and all were sharing a picnic of bread and fruit. A second girl was disrobing in the background. "Olympia" portrayed an undressed model propped up by pillows on her bed while a Negro serving-maid with a startled expression opened from its wrappings a big bouquet of flowers. At the foot of the bed a black cat with yellow eyes completed the painting's composition. The subjects were travesties, or satires, on classic art with their nymphs and nudes in sentimental surroundings. Manet did them surely with tongue in cheek, but they shocked the Parisians when he showed them. Today they hang in the Louvre, where they are world-famous.[5]

Manet had held a first one-man show in Paris, and his feeling for light and color had caught Berthe Morisot's attention. This use of light was sympathetic to her own work developed out in the sunshine under Corot's direction. So she was delighted to make a new friend in Edouard Manet. They discussed each other's paintings, and as time went on each had an influence on the other. From Manet she learned how to use broad and free brush strokes, which for years characterized the freedom of her painting. On the other hand, she urged Manet to work out of his studio, out of doors where the light was vibrant. They became exponents

of a new way of painting, begun around this time, called *plein
air,* or open air (literally, "full air").

BY THIS TIME Berthe was a fully confirmed artist. Her road
toward greatness was not marred by difficulties, or blocked by
the usual obstacles and problems. It was very slow. Progress came
step by step, from youthful apprenticeship, years of study with
Corot, and then her chance meeting with Edouard Manet.

The way of art is long for most who follow it—discouragingly
so. The overnight successes can be next day's failures. An artist
can flash into prominence, with or without background of training, and quickly be bypassed, forgotten, or at most remembered
as a slight step forward in art's history. Even so, success demands
not only long years of work. Quality, an immeasurable substance,
is essential.

Another element of success is called luck. Luck can never be
more than being in the right place at the right time. Understood
this way, luck has contributed a great deal to the ultimate success
of many artists in all fields. Yet luck has no stability without
quality, or without training.

If Berthe Morisot had not met Manet in the Louvre, would
she have been as well-known as she is today? Probably, because
the quality of her work would have erupted somewhere. Yet
that chance meeting did lead her into the circle of friends of
Manet who were thinking in the same direction. Berthe's introduction to Degas, Monet, Sisley, Rouart, Renoir came through
Manet.

An essential part of the story of Impressionism are the under-
currents that preceded it. We know to what extent average art
had degenerated into repetitious sentimentality in the early and
mid-nineteenth century. The neo-classic revival that carried Angelica Kauffmann along had worn itself out long before 1850.
The "pretty" art of people, landscapes, trees which represent that
period is seen today in museums. There were great exceptions,
Ingres for one, all the more prominent for the mediocrity around
them.

But Delacroix, Daumier, Corot and others including Turner
in England began to unloosen the chains holding art down. Not
only were they master geniuses in their own work, but their influence chipped away at public opinion and taste. After the frivol-
ity and superficiality of the French and English courts, life be-

came more realistic. As art becomes a part of history, so history is reflected in art. Those painters great enough to understand sought out a kind of "realism" in subject that was new, and a direct technique unknown since the Christian primitives.

Daumier and Delacroix showed the stark realism of people's lives. Corot, Berthe Morisot's instructor, was allied with the "Barbizon School," like Jean-Francois Millet. This school sought out a "reality" of nature and people, usually people in the country such as farmers (Millet's "The Angelus," for one). The Barbizon School preceded the Impressionists, but in reality of subject and use of outdoor sunlight they broke through the classic renderings of mythology and religious sources, and from dark color into daylight.

Another name in this early group was Gustave Courbet, born in 1819 and died in 1877. Courbet disregarded traditions, too, although not as much as his successors. As far back as 1855, two of Courbet's paintings were rejected by the International Exhibition in Paris. In furious revenge, the artist put on a one-man show of his works which he labeled "Realism," to the violent anger of his traditional opponents and an aroused public.

The paintings of these men, seen on gallery walls today, appear conservative. Not in their time. Imagine a Courbet forest now being scorned in the same manner as the wildest incursion on Madison Avenue! Yet there may have been a hundred second-rate Courbets with the same impulses who have long since faded from view. Art history repeats itself.

So these earlier innovators opened the door to the broken dots and dashes of sunlight, later used by Seurat, called "pointillism," and the clear colors of the palette from Manet.[8] It was a time of change.

Berthe Morisot, daughter of a conservative family, found herself in the center of what in equivalent terms now would be an "avant-garde." These were artists ahead of the pack, experimentalists, then rejected by the public. Today it is hard to believe that Cézanne sold few, if any, paintings in his lifetime, that Gauguin died in poverty, that Van Gogh committed suicide after painting masterpieces in an asylum. If ever there was violence and fury in art, it was during—and just before and just after—the lifetime of Berthe Morisot.

Sunlight, light in sun, light—these were madly possessed standards of the dedicated ones of the so-called Impressionists. They included as subjects the reality of things around them, a sailboat on the surface of a lake, a woman in a garden, a bowl of fruit, water lilies on a pond, a girl casually brushing her hair.[5] Subjects for paintings so commonplace were unbelievable to the public. People were used to finding in galleries of the time pictures of castles hidden among brooding mountains, of storms crashing darkly over wooded valleys, of ships at sea being tossed onto dead green rocks by dark green waves. Religious and mythological imaginings only echoed the early Renaissance. And there were always portraits, pulled painstakingly out of dark brown backgrounds of wet paint.

Instead, the Impressionists splashed and daubed their bold colors directly onto their canvases, using sweeping brush strokes or breaking color rays into fractions of separate hues. Through Edouard Manet, Berthe Morisot became one of the enthusiastic, dedicated—and very charming—members of the group.

Manet, whose name can be confused with Claude Monet, was one of the earliest to revolt openly against the academicians with his "Olympia" and "Luncheon on the Grass." In his late thirties, he was among the oldest of the group, and became, like Degas, a kind of undeclared leader. The painter friends met in one special restaurant in Paris, the Café Guerbois, 9 Avenue Clichy, usually on Friday nights. Here they could talk, argue, discuss vehemently their individual opinions, and, finally, plot the revolution. It was not a revolution against the government with arms, fighting. It was a revolution against the Art Establishment.

How much, if ever, Berthe Morisot frequented the Friday meetings at the restaurant can only be a subject of conjecture. No one knows what kind of relationship existed between Berthe Morisot and Edouard Manet. It is enough that they were close friends, that they influenced each other in their work, and that she posed for him for a number of portrait paintings. (See Plate 8.)

Manet was married, and Berthe knew his family. Six years after meeting him, she married Edouard's brother, Eugene. Once married, she gave up further posing for Edouard.

Berthe worked for the Impressionist cause, helped to organize their shows, encouraged the critics and buyers. She had a vibrant, utterly feminine and charming personality. Her home became a new gathering place for French artists and writers who were laying the foundation for a renewed glory of French culture.[8]

53

Nothing, however, kept her from painting. She did oils which reflected her own vivacity and love of life and nature. Her watercolors depicted her spontaneity as much as her subjects. Usually she worked out of doors in the sunlight, and almost always her paintings were of people. She used the expressive brush strokes which Manet, her brother-in-law, had taught her to handle. All was color: the light, the shading, the form.[24] No one quite equalled Berthe Morisot's individual style, not only fresh, clear and clean in the Impressionist way, but unique in quality because she was a woman, not a man.

Berthe took part in each of the series of Impressionist exhibitions which began with the first one of 1874, with one exception. She did not enter the 1879 show, as she had recently given birth to her daughter, Julie. Other than that she exhibited in the shows and sales which came almost annually for more than twelve years.[24]

The 1879 show, in which Berthe did not participate, was the one that marked Mary Cassatt's public debut with the Impressionists, as urged by Edgar Degas.[26]

Berthe Morisot and Mary Cassatt became close friends, working together for the common goal: acceptance of the work of their associates. Which of the two women was the better painter was not clear then, and perhaps is not now. They were different, and each very individual in style. If Mary was more forceful, Berthe was more subtle. Mary was always more careful in her drawing. Berthe for many years let color establish the forms in her work and did not concern herself with line until she was older.

Worth noting is that a third woman became identified with the group, although as a painter she never achieved significant status. She was Eve Gonzales, wife of a Paris printer. When Berthe first met Edouard Manet and posed for his portraits, she found that Eve was a model for him, too. There may have been resentment and jealousy, but Manet ignored it and continued to paint both women. All survived.

About the time of the show in 1879, and for at least three years afterward, the whole cause of Impressionism seemed to be sliding away. The paintings did not sell. Pissarro was in disastrous financial trouble. Renoir walked the streets with canvases under his arm seeking buyers. Cézanne was ignored. Manet and Degas held up their heads, but the ultimate disaster came when Durand-Ruel, the Paris art dealer who had boldly backed the group, was in financial trouble himself and reduced his purchasing for resale.[5]

If the battle seemed lost, only staunch heroism retrieved a victory. The group stood fast. Several critics began to recognize the importance of what was happening. A few buyers helped, but at the lowest—incredibly low—prices. Most of the rebel band, called now the "painters of clear color", went on to other shows in 1880, 1881 and 1882. To do them they rose from desperation.

When light might have been appearing through the clouds, it was illusory. Emile Zola, the writer, who had defended the artists of brilliant colors, turned against them. In 1880 he said that not one of these artists accomplished "with resolution and definite style the new formula. . . . They are the forerunners. . . . The man of genius is not yet born." [5]

Yet the annual shows continued. Degas went off independently. Paul Gauguin showed with the group for the first time in 1880. Then in 1883 Edouard Manet died. A memorial retrospective show of his works was given in the following year, and a few years later Claude Monet sponsored a subscription drive to purchase the painting "Olympia" as a gift to the Louvre Museum. This was the painting which had caused such a stir earlier, with the nude figure, the bunch of flowers and the black cat. A new stir was provoked, and at first the Louvre was not permitted to accept the picture. But Manet's prestige had grown, and his "Olympia" and other paintings are prizes of the Louvre today.

Berthe Morisot felt deeply the loss of Manet, her brother-in-law and friend who had introduced her into the dedicated group of dissidents. She continued showing with the group until slowly it broke apart, each artist going his own way. Berthe Morisot herself, who owed so much to the earlier advice of Edouard Manet, developed her own independent style of oil painting and watercolors, and established the lasting qualities of her own character and ability in her work.

Although she worked intensely on her painting, Berthe Morisot was always active within the ranks of her friends. She knew everyone, and it is doubtful if anyone ever spoke a critical word of her personally. With her husband Eugene Manet, who helped enthusiastically with the plans of the Impressionists, she did much to keep the group moving forward through the hard times of their public disfavor.

Berthe and Eugene Manet had a great deal to do with the last show of the Impressionists in 1886. There had been so much prior dissension that the show was nearly abandoned. But the Manets helped underwrite the expense, along with Mary Cassatt and Degas, both of whom joined their former fellow exhibitors even though they felt that their work had taken a different course. Others in that exhibition were still not selling at all. Camille Pissarro did not know from day to day where his next meal was coming from. After that show, however, the group of Impressionists split apart, and went their separate roads.

The Manets' house in Paris continued to be a social center for the active and progressive-minded participants in all the arts. The artists, writers, critics and others of congenial ideas and temperament were entertained in her home at 46 rue Paul Valery. The Manet home was filled with paintings by all of their friends, and a number of Berthe's own hung on the walls.*

Berthe Morisot's whole life was spent in energetic happiness. Like Mary Cassatt, she did not have the financial worries of many of the other painters. If she did not sell at an exhibition, it was not materially disastrous as it was to Renoir, Pissarro, and Gauguin. She was able to do what she wanted, which, more than anything, was to transform the everyday things around her into the glowing brilliance of her canvases.

Berthe Morisot did not have a one-man show of her own until after her husband died. Then, in 1892, she finally agreed to a full show of her work in Paris. The critics approved, but the public was still not used to the idea of a woman being a painter. It simply wasn't done. Successful though the show turned out to be, it did not make the spectacular imprint that it should have to have given her the reputation she deserved.

The truly heartbreaking tragedy of Berthe Morisot's life was its ending at the age of fifty-four. She died suddenly in 1895. She wrote a letter to her daughter Julie, then sixteen. One or the other must have been away from home. In part the letter read:

"My little Julie, I love you while dying; I will love you still when dead; I beg of you, do not cry; this separation was inevitable; I would have wished to go

* Berthe Morisot's daughter Julie, who married the son of Henri Rouart, another of the great Impressionists, kept the house as it was in her mother's time. Pictures loaned from that collection were exhibited in a Morisot show in Canada and in the United States in 1952 and 1953.

*when you were married . . . Work and be good as you
have always been; you have never caused me a sorrow
in your little life. You have beauty, fortune; make good
use of them. I think it best that you live with your cousins, rue de Villejust, but I impose nothing on you. You
will give a remembrance of me to your Aunt Edma and
to your cousins; to your cousin Gabriel, the "Boats under
Repair" of Monet. You will say to Monsieur Degas that
if he founds a museum, he should choose a Manet. A
remembrance to Monet, to Renoir and a drawing of
mine to Bartholomé.* Give to the two concierges. Do not
cry; I love you even more than I embrace you. . . ."* [24]

The following day Berthe Morisot died. She is buried in the
tomb of the Manet family in the Parisian cemetery of Passy.

IT IS inevitable that Berthe Morisot and Mary Cassatt should be
compared one with the other. In many respects they were remarkably alike, by coincidence. Yet in the final analysis of their
work they were very different.

As girls, they came from similar backgrounds even though
one was French and one was American. They were "young ladies"
of whom the last thing expected was that they would become
identified with unknown art revolutionaries. Their minds were
attuned; both dedicated every thought and interest toward painting. Independently, they chose the same basic ideas of painting:
in technique, a freedom of palette and color and light that was
in direct opposition to the accepted normals of the time, in subject, a rejection of the traditional and a finding of life in the
commonplace. This was especially so with people. Perhaps more
than any of the other Impressionist School, the two women
painters found their themes in ordinary people.

Renoir painted sensual nudes in living colors as well as little
children, with mothers or nannies, in pretty party-like dresses.
Degas did dancers in their school and on stage. Edouard Manet
painted people as well as still-lifes and water scenes, but his
characters seem, curiously, more planned than true, however well
done. Gauguin, later, placed his human subjects as part of a

---

* Paul-Albert Bartholomé was another Impressionist, friend of Berthe
Morisot and Mary Cassatt, better known in those days than he
is now.

decorative composition, beautifully. Claude Monet was more concerned with experimentation with light and color innovations and discoveries. Pissarro turned to landscapes. These were great masters, each one, and the world has long recognized their supreme perception of their art.

Yet both women, contemporary to them, found a kind of personal relationship to their particular subjects for which the men would not have thought to look. This is the difference that a woman can feel, a kind of sympathetic planting of herself in the subject being painted.

Gauguin was only one of those who agreed that both women were charming, but Mary Cassatt had more force. Here is the difference between the two. Whereas Mary Cassatt had a strong, sometimes impatient or even demanding personality, Berthe Morisot was essentially gentle and sympathetic.

Berthe's education in art came faster, earlier, and more direct to her. To study for six years under an active Corot brought a different experience than Mary's first student frustrations and the later self-discipline of study of old masters in the museums. Berthe was about twenty-seven when she met and came under the influence of Edouard Manet. Mary had passed thirty when she met Degas. There was a great difference in the warm personality of Manet and the sharp criticism of Degas. Each man seems to have matched the potentials of the girls in their respective ways. Manet's advice was good for Berthe, and brought out all her budding ability. Degas, too, was good for Mary Cassatt, and he pulled her from reveries and adoration of the past into the opportunities of the present.

Berthe Morisot remained an Impressionist from her first introduction by Manet to uninhibited freedom in expressing form. One of the concepts of Impressionism was the breaking down of carefully detailed forms into loose areas of color and light. The painting counted, not the subject. Before that time artists had fallen into the habit of copying their models, or still-lifes or landscapes, believing that the truth lay in what they saw before them. The Impressionists opened the doors by proving that the truth lay in the painting itself, as an instrument of the artist's self-expression. The model would go away and be forgotten. The painting remained.

Nevertheless, at least five years before she died, Berthe Morisot began to question her own technique in painting. Were the free and wide sweeps of the brush enough to capture the essence of the subject? She began to use more specific delineation of form, a greater reliance on line as a symbol for its purpose. Her technique changed, and an ability to draw well suddenly became more useful than it had been for years. Berthe Morisot moved forward a long step, and the sharper character of forms in her painting is clear from her one-man exhibition in 1892. She never came to the intense self-discipline in drawing that Mary Cassatt undertook. Yet Berthe was still developing this new concept when she died. How much more, even, might she have achieved?

Nevertheless, Berthe Morisot left a legacy of oil paintings that few men have surpassed for quality, for feeling, and for that intangible substance that makes works of art great. She not only aided and added to a fantastic era of violent change, but she entered into the ranks of the great painters of all time.

Not long ago John Canaday of *The New York Times* summarized the meaning of Berthe Morisot by writing in his critic's column these words:

"Surely the freshest exhibition in New York at the moment is Berthe Morisot's, although this enchanting impressionist died sixty-five years ago. The seventy canvases assembled at Wildenstein's . . . in a show opening today are the largest exhibition of her work ever held in the United States, and should extend the list of conquests that this most irresistibly feminine of painters has been making for three generations."

Each of these seven women in this book has a portrait of herself included in the reproductions. Four of them are self-portraits. The other three women are each represented by portraits done by others.

MANET'S
PORTRAIT

Mary Cassatt was painted by Edgar Degas (Plate 11). Berthe Morisot, appears in a painting by Edouard Manet (Plate 8).

No coincidence occurred in the selection for reproduction here of a painting of Berthe Morisot by Edouard Manet, and of Mary Cassatt by Edgar Degas. The two women were close friends in Paris. Both were closely identified with Impressionism. So were the men, although each distinctly individual.

Manet's portrait was done in 1869, about a year after he had met Berthe studying in the Louvre. She was twenty-eight, and Manet thirty-seven. It is not within the province of this book to analyze the painting here by Edouard Manet, or later the one by

Degas. Yet a comment is in order, especially in comparing the portraits by the two painters.

Manet has caught the essence of femininity which was Berthe's, in a way which implies also his own spirited personality. Her piquant nose, her sparkling eyes, the delicacy of features show her as the vivacious woman she was. The curl over her forehead must have been typical. Even the hat, the fur coat and muff are a part of herself. The colors are in variations of brown, following the tone established by the rich darkness of the fur. The technique is a typical example of Impressionism. Instead of a formal portrait establishing every detail, the painting is done freely, suggestively.

Edouard Manet fully caught Berthe's lovely qualities.

HER OWN
WORK

BERTHE MORISOT's "Mother and Sister of the Artist" is dated 1869–1870 and reveals clearly its origin in the earlier part of her career. The portrait lacks the vivacity of the later manner as acquired from Manet. The painting certainly is not conservative for that day. It is done simply, with freshness and some perception of the wide subtleties of composition. The drawing is superb.

Yet the portrait of the two so-close members of her family does not indicate the Impressionist mood of color for its own sake, in portraits or landscape. It carries the stamp of an older generation, undoubtedly that of Corot, her instructor for so many years. Her mother's dark conservative dress compares knowingly with her youthful sister's light gown. So does the bright design of the sofa, an offset to the full dark skirt. The picture frame, squared, and the tabletop, rounded, are done with understanding of the solution to a completed composition. Guidance and training bring an artist to know these things. Intuition helps, but it is not enough.

Berthe nevertheless made two errors in the composition of this painting. One is so minor as to be questionable, and the intention almost excuses the error. The piece of paper or book on the tabletop, running out of the left side of the picture, is almost exactly centered. In composition, centering a line or form on any edge is academically wrong. The practice usually breaks the overall togetherness, and in this case the paper seems to do just that. But Berthe put the form of the light-colored paper there to hold the composition. Remove it, and the whole por-

PLATE 9

The Mother and Sister of the Artist, by Berthe Morisot.
National Gallery of Art, Washington, D.C.,
Chester Dale Collection

trait collapses. The paper is justified, but its centering in the middle of the left margin is not. It could have been better placed slightly lower, thereby bringing the whole tabletop lower. The change might have necessitated a change in composition elsewhere in the painting, probably in the picture frame, but it would have been worth the extra study.

Why carp over so small a thing in a beautifully executed painting? Simply because small things distract the eye and attention, even subconsciously. A great painter misses nothing except intentionally—and an intentional miss is not a miss at all. Berthe Morisot was a great painter, and it is unlikely that she would have repeated this centered form later on.

Her other error in this picture is more clearly a mistake in planning. The fingers of the left hand in her lap, the outside line of the right arm coming forward, and the right side of the table all meet together in exactly the same place. In making a painting, this meeting of forms with edges so close is something to be avoided. It seems to distract attention from the painting itself. It creates a disturbing and annoying element, even if one is not really aware of the cause. In this painting Berthe Morisot should have been more aware of basic composition, and either moved the tabletop back slightly away from the hand and arm or let the top overlap these latter forms just enough to break the precise juxtaposition.

The painting does contain an especially interesting element for speculation. What is the subject of the picture on the wall? Nothing is clearly definable. The forms work into the whole composition of the portrait. Berthe realized that vagueness in doing the framed picture on the wall was essential. If she had made a definite "picture within a picture," every eye would have looked at that out of curiosity, and passed over the portraits of her mother and sister. The vagueness she used appears almost abstract. Yet "abstract" art was not created for many years after this painting was made. A curious thought is that Berthe Morisot, in using general elements of design in her picture on the wall rather than a defined subject unwittingly approached the idea of abstraction, far ahead of its time. The difference, of course, is that she did not use lack of definition of a realistic subject as an end in itself. It was intended only as a tool in the creation of the whole composition.

The painting, "In the Dining Room," dated 1886 (Color Plate 2), shows Berthe Morisot at the height of her power. It is painted with freedom from restrictions of any kind, filled with color without the necessity for literal explanations. It is gay, declaring the enthusiasm of a bright morning. The girl is happy, and the little dog plays cheerfully on the floor at her feet.

The painting suggests rather than delineates. The style is typical of Berthe Morisot's work until she changed in later years to more specific drawing.

One remembers that the intention of Impressionism was to break away from the time-worn literal exactness which characterized the traditionalists. When Berthe painted this dining room interior, she was in the forefront of revolution. This is the kind of art which shocked and enraged the Paris conservatives. The suggestive technique freed art from its previous bonds and set the pace for the "modern" that followed.

Nevertheless, Berthe Morisot followed closely the discipline of composition, without which even the most radical work of art by any measure falls apart. She was more concerned with the composition of the colors than with a definition of space. There is little to give illusion to the depth of the room, only a minor use of perspective lines: the chair is placed obviously behind the girl, and its drawing gives some idea of space. So do the lines of the sideboard, especially across the top where the point of the cornice helps to throw the back wall into place.

On the other hand, the colors themselves are mostly of equal strength or value. They hold to the same relative "plane," and do not push themselves back or pull forward for the sake of defining space. Colors considered alone, the picture is practically two-dimensional. This in itself was a major break with traditional painting, where "cool" colors were supposed to recede, and "warm" colors move out. "In the Dining Room" shows the fallacy of theories.

The blues of the girl's dress and jacket are predominant, but picked up in response all through the painting, in darks and lights. The other basic color used here is the variable red-orange ochre, primarily in the large rectangle of the open sideboard door. If the eye sees the panel first, it is at once pulled to the girl's hair of the same color, then briefly to the house rooftops through the window in the upper right hand corner, but promptly back again to the girl's head and face, the focal point of the painting. Other suggestions of the same basic color are placed here and there for balance, even on the dog's ear. The chair adds, too. The fruit on the table, slight though it seems, holds that large open door in place. If one's finger is placed for a moment over the fruit to eliminate it, the whole picture changes. Try it.

So each area of color is balanced by another, and still by others.

The forms of objects in the painting carry out the same relation of one to another. The tall figure of the girl is clearly made taller by the upward lines of the French doors, held in turn where they belong by the chair under them. The chair, on the other hand, seems to pull attention over to the right margin, but the full-length section of wall up the whole right side of the painting turns the eye direction once more past the table to the rooftops, from where it again jumps to the girl's hair and face.

That oversized panel of the open door is counteracted by the window square above the girl's head, to the right. Its size is also diminished by the broken colors and lines of the upper part of the cabinet. It is easy now to find squares and rectangles all through the painting, including the flat one of the chair seat.

Rounded forms are present, too, each in relation to the other. The table top is first, then the half circle of the hem of the girl's skirt, and the clock on the wall. It is possible to keep on finding forms that answer forms, colors that balance colors.

Not one line, not one variation of color, not one form in Berthe Morisot's painting is done by accident. Take out the least part of the whole, and the balance is changed. The hinge line of the door is an example. Was it casually placed there? Not at all. See the painting without it, and what happens?

Even the forward tilt of the cupboard in the upper left corner is important in containing the painting within its limits. And the cupboard is held up by the opposing backward slant of the chair.

This is Composition, with a capital "C." The necessity of a work of art is to create a wholeness within itself. The eye may see everything in the first moment, but then it lights on a certain place and from there to another and on until it rests finally on the focal point. Each move is intended by the artist, the skilled artist who understands how to set up a situation and then solve it.

How does an artist make the gaze of someone looking at his painting move from place to place at his own will? This requires study, intuition and understanding. For example, ordinarily a viewer's eye will enter a painting from the lower right hand corner, cross to the left, and move upward. Why? This is a puzzle for psychiatry. In her painting, "In the Dining Room," Berthe Morisot knew this, and used the guide line of the shadow across the floor to capitalize on it (bypassing the dog, which is seen only later). A painter can deliberately reverse the path by providing an avenue in from the left hand corner. Or he can cancel natural instinct by placing a form or color in some other area to catch the eye first.

In interpreting and understanding the work of a skilled artist, it is rewarding to make particular note of how he has handled the eye's travel path through his painting, to focus at last on the one central and final area.

One more comment should be made about this painting of Morisot's. She learned, as already pointed out, the use of free wide brush strokes from her friend and guide, Manet. Look again at the door panel, at the girl's apron, and the panes of the French doors. There is Manet's influence.

A change of pace by Berthe Morisot is seen in the very simple watercolor painting, "A Lady in a Park" (Plate 10). The painting itself is small, only seven-and-a-half by eight-and-three-sixteenth inches. It may be assumed that it was done on the spot, quickly and freely, on a small sketch pad. Slight though it appears in reproduction, the essential qualities of composition are still there.

This time the scarcely suggested slats of a bench pull the eye in from the left, across the girl's figure, to the open parasol. From it, attention is led by the arc of trees past the vague indication of other people to the girl's hat and then to her face, the ultimate point to which everything in the painting leads.

The lines, designs and pattern of this brief composition show again how Berthe Morisot understood so well the technique of painting that she could use it subconsciously. Others use technique too, but she went further than most, to create from her own lively personality joyful masterpieces of art.

PLATE 10

A Lady in a Park: watercolor by Berthe Morisot.
The Metropolitan Museum of Art, New York,
Harris Brisbane Dick, 1948.

Madame Grand, later Princesse de Talleyrand-Périgord,
by Elisabeth Louise Vigée-Lebrun
The Metropolitan Museum of Art, New York,
bequest of Edward S. Harkness, 1940.

COLOR PLATE 2

In the Dining Room, by Berthe Morisot.
*National Gallery of Art, Washington, D.C.,
Chester Dale Collection.*

The Boating Party, by Mary Cassatt.
National Gallery of Art, Washington, D.C.,
Chester Dale Collection

COLOR PLATE 4

Child in a Straw Hat, by Mary Cassatt.
From the collection of Mr. and Mrs. Paul Mellon.

Man with the Cat (Henry Sturgis Drinker), by Cecilia Beaux.
Henry Ward Ranger Fund Collection,
Smithsonian Institution, Washington, D.C.

COLOR PLATE 6

Les Deux Amies, by Marie Laurencin.
From the collection of the Wally F. Galleries,
New York.

COLOR PLATE 7

Wave, Night, by Georgia O'Keeffe.
*Addison Gallery of American Art,
Phillips Academy, Andover.*

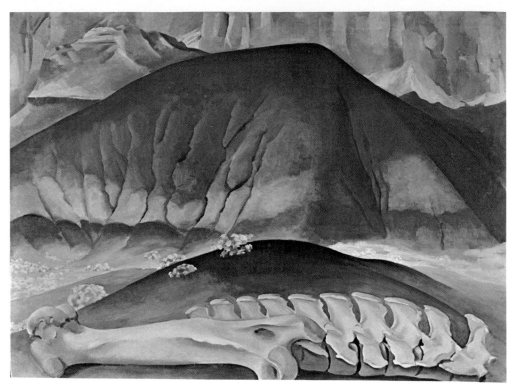

COLOR PLATE 8

Red Hills and Bones, 1941, by Georgia O'Keeffe.
Philadelphia Museum of Art:
The Alfred Stieglitz Collection.

CHAPTER 5

Mary Cassatt

1844–1926

T IS A strange twist that, of the few truly great women painters historically, two should have exhibited together, and become involved with the same group of dissident art revolutionists. It was partly coincidence that brought Mary Cassatt and Berthe Morisot together in Paris, and also it was inevitable through their own kindred interests. The individual genius of each carried them both to greatness among the Impressionists.

How did an American girl come to be accepted as an equal by those fiery Frenchmen who have since become immortal—aside from the monetary value of their work? Mary Cassatt was born in 1844—three years after Berthe Morisot's birth—in Allegheny City, Pennsylvania, across the river from Pittsburgh and now part of it, a most unlikely place for the birth of a great artist. She was fifth in a family of seven children, a family with reasonably solid financial background.[26] Yet her father was restless, and never quite achieved the status of a successful businessman for all his social prestige. Her mother, fortunately for Mary, loved Europe, and managed to take her family abroad for a long stay while her daughter was still young. Meantime, the Cassatt family had moved to Philadelphia, which, for Mary, was as much of a home base in America as she had.

After some years in Europe, the Cassatts returned to the United States, and Mary received the proper education for a young and established socialite. Her father shifted residence from Philadelphia to the suburbs, from one house to another.[26] Somewhere along the way, Mary began to consider painting.

In those days, and indeed very long after, a respectable girl with social background was expected to follow the usual conventions. Home was the place to be, practicing the requirements for a good wife and mother. She was supposed to follow demurely the accepted social entertainments until she was married. Mary was not an ordinary society girl. The idea of a career in art haunted her, far out of reach though it surely was at that point.

Mary must have had her mother's sympathy in the pursuit of her dreams. Mrs. Cassatt was not so conventional herself that she did not yearn for the broader life of Europe, and close ties kept mother and daughter together over long years. She must have understood Mary's already strong spirit.

At that time in Philadelphia, the Pennsylvania Academy of the Fine Arts maintained a school for painters. It was—and is now—the oldest art school in America, as well as an art museum, established as far back as 1805 by Charles Willson Peale, the head of an entire family devoted to art. The Academy had lived through disasters, the last at that time being a ravaging fire which destroyed its building and ruined its precious collection of French plaster casts sent to it as its first art collection by Nicholas Biddle, one of the earliest ambassadors to France.[9] The original casts were made from Greek sculpture pieces taken from Italy by Napoleon, and reproduced under the direction of the French sculptor Houdon. The loss in the end might have been appreciated by students of the school, because the common practice at that time was to learn drawing from the plaster reproductions before using a live model—a custom at which the great Greek sculptors surely would have shuddered. But the plaster casts were replaced, and when Mary Cassatt was allowed by her father to enter the Academy as a student, "antique" drawing was routine. So was copying paintings by masters.

Mary did not object to learning by copying the work of others. She did it later, in Italy, from the great paintings of Correggio. She did not want specific instruction and rejected it in Paris after a brief try.

Much later in life, Mary Cassatt told a French interviewer: "A l'ecole Academique de Philadelphie on dessinait tant bien que mal d'apres des copies anciennes ou des plâtres antiques. Il n'y

PLATE 11

Portrait of Mary Cassatt, by Edgar Degas.
André Meyer Collection.

avait pas d'enseignment. Je crois d'ailleurs que la peinture ne s'enseigne pas, et qu'un n'a pas besoin de suivre les lecons d'un maitre. L'enseignement des musees suffit." [28] *At the Academy School of Philadelphia one drew so much better after classic copies or from antique plasters. There was no teaching there. I think moreover that painting is not taught, and that one does not need to follow the lessons of a teacher. The teaching of museums is sufficient.*

At the time when Mary Cassatt was a student at the Pennsylvania Academy during the Civil War, the school had in its enrollment between 300 and 400 persons.[30] How many were part-time students is difficult to know. The plaster casts to which Mary refers were kept in a dark attic on South Penn Square. Students had considerable difficulty in finding light and space for drawing. Not until some five years later was drawing from the live model opened to women at all.

Even long after Mary Cassatt's student days at the Academy, life classes for drawing and painting from models were divided so that men and women never mixed in working from the nude figure.[30] Entrance to life classes was severely restricted. Copying from older paintings in the museum was a basic course, but permission had to be obtained first from the Directors, who carefully specified that the copy had to be smaller than the original.[9]

The records indicate that Mary Cassatt was a student at the Pennsylvania Academy for four years, although the files are not clear on how much time she actually worked there.[9] From her own enthusiasm for art, it can be inferred that she spent much time on the Academy precincts, even while living in the country with somewhat infrequent trips to town. Whether from the Academy or from her later experiences in Paris, she did develop an aversion not to the classic masters, but to the administrators and jurymen who set themselves up as arbiters of artistic judgment always from the conservative viewpoint.

In her older years, when Mary Cassatt finally came to be accepted as a great American painter, she remained so firmly opposed to the art "Organization" that she refused every prize and honor awarded to her, the great exception being the Gold Medal of the Pennsylvania Academy of the Fine Arts. This she did accept and acknowledge as well might a student of the Academy schools who had gained such recognition in the art world.

By an odd chance, it seems that Mary Cassatt was an Academy student during the same four years when Thomas Eakins studied there, from 1861 through 1864. Both were to achieve eminence in American art, different as were their styles and feelings. After school, their careers went separate ways. Eakins spent four years in Paris—enough for his temperament—and returned to Philadelphia for the rest of his life. Mary Cassatt went to Europe and worked there untiringly through long years until age prevented her from continuing.

As classmates at the Pennsylvania Academy they must have known each other well, even though Academy records show a total of 352 students registered in the year 1862.[9] It was a large school for that time. Eakins is considered now by many as the foremost American painter to this day. Few will dispute that Mary Cassatt has been the greatest woman painter the United States produced, and her achievements make use of the word "woman" almost derogatory. Beyond their background of age and schooling, Eakins and Cassatt had little in common except that both thought and expressed themselves in the world of ordinary human beings, catching normal, living people in everyday life in their masterpieces of perception. And both were in rebellion against restrictions and prejudice. While Mary Cassatt joined the Impressionists in Paris, Eakins—as head of the Pennsylvania Academy schools in later years—was forced to resign for his unorthodox methods of teaching, which were frowned upon by the staid Academy directors.

According to her French biographer, Mary Cassatt decided to become a painter in 1868. She was twenty-four, and this was a good four years after her Academy studies. Meanwhile, she had made another trip to Paris with her mother. What makes anyone decide to be an artist? The decision, in her case as well as in so many others, was irrevocable. As a decision, it was deadly serious—not one made in art school where she might have been killing time doing something she enjoyed until she married. It was a mature decision, arrived at after experience and travel.

To decide to become a painter—and even the word in this sense has a meaning of complete dedication of self and life—was one thing for a man, such as Eakins. For a woman it was difficult in those years. Women did not decide to become professional painters; it wasn't "done." Mary's decision was compounded by the fact that her family was socially correct, and

71

even more by her being a Philadelphian. Even today in Philadelphia one is supposed to do the "correct" thing, although the precept may be more broken than kept.

With her decision to become a painter, Mary announced to her family her plans of going first to Italy, alone. The story is, without any proven foundation, that her father said at one point that he would rather see her dead than pursue painting as a career. This may or may not be true. An obvious guess is that he had doubts about his daughter traveling by herself to Europe, with every intention of remaining there. But his doubts must have been dispelled later, when he moved to Paris with his wife and younger children to follow his serious-minded daughter.

Mary first went to Parma, in northern Italy. On her way, she surely had doubts herself about her decision, although Mary Cassatt was growing more intuitive and knowing about art. She was leaving behind a life of society, entertainment, ease and security to make her own way in a foreign country. She was always prone to seasickness on the ocean. That feeling of sureness in herself and her instinct about art sustained her, and she did have enough money to be free from worry.

In Parma she found the works of the north Italian Correggio, the late Renaissance painter who lived in the early 1500's, and who was neither a part of the Venetian School of painting nearby, nor of the Florentine or Sienese Schools further south. He was an individualist by himself, with dramatic paintings of people, filled with the technical knowledge of composition and the glory of color. "What a master!" she exclaimed.[28] She studied his work for eight months, and then traveled to Spain where she saw the masterpieces of Peter Paul Rubens in the Prado Museum. First sight was enough. She moved on from Madrid to Antwerp, where she could absorb all the knowledge and technique of Rubens as if he were a living teacher instead of a painter dead nearly two hundred and forty years. His feelings of form and color, the beauty of flesh and lights were as real as if he himself had been at her elbow to explain his ideals. She spent a summer with the masterpieces of Rubens to teach her.

During months of self-study Mary Cassatt's reputation grew, amazing for any beginner. From Rome, where she went from Holland, she sent a painting to the annual Salon of Paris and it was accepted. This was a painting which she had previously done at Parma, one of her first in Europe, which she called "During the Carnival," a painting definitely under the influence of her Correggio studies. The French Salon was the basic home of the traditionalists, and to be accepted for its exhibitions was the greatest honor a young painter could receive. This was in 1872 and Mary Cassatt was twenty-eight.

The following year her entry to the Salon was again accepted. This was the painting, now famous, "Offering the Drink to the Bullfighter," showing a young girl handing refreshment to a brightly costumed toreador. Its subject reflected her stay in Spain. The third year she was successful again, with a head painted in Rome, in the tradition of Rubens.

According to the story told, Edgar Degas went to see that Salon show, and stopped in front of the painting by Mary Cassatt. He is reported to have said, "This is real. There is someone who feels as I do."[28]

Mary Cassatt was living in the clouds. She moved to Paris permanently. Then the bubble burst. In the following year the Salon rejected a portrait of her sister Lydia.[27] It was a bitter reversal, enough to make anyone but an artist dedicated to art and to her future give up.

Mary described her own emotions in a letter which she wrote to a friend and one-time fellow student in Philadelphia:

> *"Did mother tell you of my misfortune last spring. I did not get in the Salon. My picture, Mr. Frère said, was infinitely better than last year's, but it was large and not sufficiently finished."* She blamed herself for this, up to a point. *"I was very much pressed for time and therefore was not very surprised at my fate, although of course I felt dreadfully about it. Well, Rourge was also refused on both of hers, both infinitely better than last year's, but Mr. Frère got one in for her. So you see they are not so very just after all. Mr. Gerome was very kind to me for when I heard that I was refused I went to him but alas! it was too late. He told me if I had come twenty-four hours sooner he would have got my picture through! . . . After I had heard my fate I went into Paris and stayed there three months, but did little work, in fact none at all. I was not very well and of course very much discouraged. . . ."*[33]

So every artist learns the hard way the bitterness of rejection.

Mary toned down the colors of the same painting for a re-submission in the following year's Salon. This time it was accepted. Her anger and disillusionment at this dictatorial control of taste were complete. She never again showed in the Salon.

Yet Mary Cassatt was not the kind to give up. No true artist can be. It was simply that she had not yet found herself.

EDGAR DEGAS

IN THE early days of the Impressionists the name of Degas was laughable to Parisians. A painter of ballet dancers wilting on their feet like faded flowers, of stage scenes with swirling skirts of jumbled colors, of horse races that anyone could see with their own eyes instead of in what were reputed to be paintings! A painter! An artist!

Among the ridiculed group of the Impressionists, Edgar Degas, somewhat older, temperamental, irascible, moody, unfriendly, was one of the leaders. Impressionism, much like the often-repeated warnings beforehand of a volcano's explosion, had been preceded by Courbet, Manet, and older painters who were feeling their way into something new. Degas was one of these.

A friend brought Degas one day to Mary Cassatt's studio. She had known his paintings. She had seen the early Impressionist shows. She perceived in what they were doing a groping toward what she was attempting: the use of light color, of subjects that were commonplace and at hand. But a gulf separated her from the group. She did not know them, and they could not have known her.

Degas' visit changed her life. He saw her work, and liked it. Perhaps he remembered her painting in the Salon show which caused him to say that she thought as he did. They became immediate friends, and from then on Degas' criticism of her paintings brought out all that was intuitive and self-learned in her ability.

He told her never to submit again to the Salon, but asked her to join the Impressionists and show with them. There would not be a jury to say no, there would not be a limitation on personal expression. Joyfully Mary accepted.[28]

"At last I could work with absolute independence without worrying myself about the final opinion of a jury!" she said. "I hated conventional art! I began to live!"[28]

Mary had joined in a battle, a French battle, of which at that moment she could not have realized the worldwide significance. The battle was between the traditionalists, the romantics, the painters consecrated to historical works, and those who sought a new sincerity in nature, of light, of new techniques and colors on their palettes. Not only painting was involved, but literature, too.

The fight was in earnest, and in the fourth show of the Impressionists, in 1879, in an empty apartment rented for the occasion, the work of Mary Cassatt was included with oil paintings and pastels. Some of the other exhibitors were Degas, Forain, Monet, Pissarro, Rouart—all today French modern classicists.[28]

That an American woman, then thirty-five, could have had clarity of mind to align herself with the radical group was one of the first evidences of her remarkable judgment. To her, faith in these painters was not extraordinary. In the museums she had found the master painters she liked, Correggio, Rubens, others. She saw instinctively their relationship to life, to feeling, and their use of color. Even before she met Degas, she could feel that he, too, was a master like them. She understood what the Paris critics and public did not see, that Degas, and those with him, were successors to the classic master painters. It was a natural step for her to follow Degas.

Nothing indicates that she was even his pupil. Yet she did accept his work as she had that of Correggio and Rubens.

Edgar Degas never married. He considered the idea a number of times, but was uncertain of the effect a possible wife's ideas would have on his work. Probably Mary Cassatt's was the closest friendship he ever had with a woman. He was ten years older. They remained close friends, and when Degas had trouble finding the right model for his paintings (i.e., "At the Milliner's," now in the Metropolitan Museum of Art, New York), Mary posed for him.[27] Mary never married, either; her art was her life. The two were friends for forty years, but not always steadily. Both had strong personalities, and often they clashed. When they did, six months or more might go by without their seeing each other. Then something brought them together again —Degas found one of her paintings in a gallery which he liked so much that he rushed back to her, or she had a question on which she needed an answer. She was in fact his disciple.

75

Whatever their truly personal relationship was is lost. She destroyed his letters to her before her death.[27] All the time she knew him she was afraid of his criticism, that it might discourage her. Yet between the two, Degas and Cassatt, there remained that closeness that he is supposed to have expressed before they ever met, when he first saw her painting: "She thinks as I do."

Degas' temperament was not like Mary's. He was to the outside world a rough, caustic, vitriolic man entirely unlike the shadow who has been supposed to haunt the wings of the Paris Opera and Ballet School like a wan ghost catching *les petites danseuses* at practice or at rest. He was a leader of the Impressionists, even though in the final analysis he differed in style from them, as Mary Cassatt did, too. But at heart Edgar Degas had a tenderness, a feeling of sympathy, a sentiment that perhaps was one thing that brought him close to the American woman painter whom he respected.

During this time of Mary's change from conventional art to the then-radical, her family followed her to Paris. Her mother and father moved over from Philadelphia, with her sister Lydia who had already been with her abroad at one time or another. Her father gave up his Philadelphia work, and lived on what he had. Mary's brother, Alexander Cassatt, who had gone into the railroad business, became more and more successful in Philadelphia until he finally became head of the Pennsylvania Railroad. He could and did help his family.

To say that Mary Cassatt was wealthy through her background and needed nothing is not true. The Cassatts were never in real financial trouble, and Mary could run a household of servants to put on parties for the most distinguished Frenchmen of the art and literary world. Yet she still had to be careful, and even her father in Paris demanded that her studio pay for itself, what with costs of models and materials. Mary's family was a burden to her—which surely she would never have admitted —and a tragic burden. The Cassatt family remained with her in Europe, and despite some traveling and summers spent away, they made Paris their headquarters.

Then her sister Lydia died, and her father, and after long years in Mary's care until old age, her mother.

Even before she became formally associated with the French Impressionists, Mary Cassatt did not forget that she was an

American. She exhibited in the Pennsylvania Academy of the Fine Arts Annual show in 1876, this being the year that the new building (the present one at Broad and Cherry Streets) was opened. The new Academy was in time for the nation's Centennial in Philadelphia the same year. She was in the Academy show again in 1878 and in 1879; and in 1878 she had a painting in the Annual Exhibition of the National Academy of Design in New York.[26]

It seems that these paintings of Mary Cassatt's were the first Impressionist paintings introduced to the United States.[26] They were reasonably accepted by a few, but America did not realize for many years longer what their leading art representative in France, woman or not, was doing.

MARY CASSATT's real introduction into the world of great art was her representation in that Impressionist show of 1879 in Paris.

She exhibited a painting called "La Loge," a girl in a box at the opera, smiling and holding a fan. The drawing was superb, the feeling and composition of the highest quality. Degas was then beginning to make theater subjects popular. Although the Paris critics blasted most of the show, they could not truly resent the work of Cassatt. To her and to Degas himself went their grudging compliments. To the others exhibiting, they were not complimentary.

The public came to laugh, but 17,000 people did pay to see the show. They bought almost nothing. Some of the painters wanted to hold the slight profits for future show expenses, but the majority decided to split among the exhibitors at once. With the small proceeds Mary Cassatt bought a work by Degas and another by Monet.[28]

The next Impressionist show was held the following year. Berthe Morisot was with her. This was the show where Paul Gauguin is supposed to have remarked about the two women, "Mademoiselle Cassatt has as much charm, but she has more force." [28]

Mary did indeed have force, of personality, of intensity for work, of opinion. She was humble in character, yet strong and implacable in her resolve. She yielded to Degas, who could criticize her mercilessly. She respected Manet. She was influenced to a degree by Renoir, the great master who so remarkably found the subtleties of the female figure. Yet Cassatt sought always her own individuality, based on her convictions.

She was still Mary Cassatt, the American, with the will-power and strength of her pioneer ancestors.

THE DIVISION OF THE IMPRESSIONISTS

IT WAS impossible to anticipate that a group of artists with bold and radical ideas of their own could hold themselves together as one bloc very long. It was remarkable that an assortment of a dozen to a dozen and a half painters who had been labeled "Impressionists" could remain a close-knit circle for twelve years which they managed to do. Finally, however, individualism came out. Independence of style and technique, personal ideas and the needs to follow their own roads brought the so-called Impressionists to the dividing point. After all, most of them have long since been called geniuses in their own right.

In part, the division was brought about by increasing recognition among Paris art critics and among keen buyers who realized that some of these painters who defied conventional art did have ability and something to say in a new way. In the beginning, the painters had been somewhat like the animals in Noah's ark; they came together in common self-protection against the flood of angry public opinion. When the storm showed signs of subsiding they came forth to follow again their natural impulses. The lions roared at the tigers, the cats ate the mice. The artists did not eat each other, but they—many of them—moved into their own orbits of self-expression.

Degas was one. He had not, from the beginning, liked the title of Impressionist. He preferred Independent. Independent he was and his work showed it. He reached the point when he decided not to show his paintings with the Impressionist group. Mary Cassatt followed him out, at least for one show, to the distress of some of the others who remained.*

Meanwhile, Mary was doing much soul-searching of her own work. She had achieved a high degree of color sense and composition in her pictures. Yet she felt that she had not reached the full depth of feeling that characterized the art of the great masters, classic as well as contemporary. Part of what she needed, she felt, was greater facility in drawing and definition of form.[28] She worked more intensely on dry point etchings and aquatint prints, the kind of work that permits not the slightest er-

* See last section on Berthe Morisot.

rors of line or definition of form.* In daylight hours she painted. At night she drew.

Much happened through the next years of Mary's continuing work. There were interruptions. It was through this period that her loved sister, Lydia, who had posed for many of her paintings, died in Paris. Her mother was not well. Mary took her to a better climate in Spain for the greater part of a winter. Other members of the Cassatt family came to Paris to visit from the United States. All her life she had loved horseback riding, and in Paris kept a horse of her own. One day, in 1888, she fell and broke her leg. This prevented her from riding again.[26]

Yet nothing kept her long from work. The next factor in her development, and a major influence on many French painters, too, was an exhibition in Paris in 1890 of Japanese prints.

Most artists had some previous familiarity with the art of Japan, new though it was. Only in 1853 had Commodore Perry and his Navy vessels "discovered" Japan for the West. It took some years for Japanese art to be discovered, too, and even longer for it to be exported. Degas knew about it, and he told Mary Cassatt. He was one of the earliest to perceive the simplicity of Japanese line, the superb composition of their forms and colors, and the Oriental feeling. When the 1890 exhibition of prints came to Paris, a whole new wave of inspiration swept over the discerning French artists.

Mary Cassatt and Degas went to a dinner party together and then to the Exhibition. Later she went with Berthe Morisot.[26]

From then on Mary intensified her print making, inspired by the Japanese but using always her own expressiveness in subject matter and in technique. By this time Mary Cassatt was in her fifties. She had no fear of adopting changes into her work. She continually grew in depth.

And slowly not only her work but also that of the others who had started out as Impressionists began to be more accepted everywhere. An Impressionist show in London attracted much interest, even if little liked by the public. Other shows were introduced in America, in New York and in Boston. The financial results were poor, but new ideas were planted.

In 1891 Mary Cassatt had her first one-man show at the gallery of Durand-Ruel, the famous international dealer who did much

MARY'S
LATER CAREER

*See further on "Interpretation of Mary Cassatt's Work."

to build up the early Impressionist group.[28] She had not before then felt ready for this momentous step in the life of any artist.

To hold a one-man show is for a painter, or a sculptor, like being a singer or a pianist on stage all alone the first time for an entire evening's performance. There is no one else to distract attention. The critics come with skepticism, and to keep their own reputations. Many of them feel that they must play to the galleries by finding fault and expressing personal prejudices. The serious and earnest critics are rightly critical. Collectors pause to wonder whether they ought to pick up bargains. The public waits, looking as much at the reactions of other people as they look at the paintings, ready to praise or scoff on someone else's cue. A first one-man exhibition is to an artist terrifying, and the critical reaction can be devastating to a career. Sometimes even the finest artists need years to recover from a failure of their first personal public showing.

Mary Cassatt knew these things. She approached timidly, and used only five oil paintings and twelve prints—a small group for a one-man show. Camille Pissarro, another of the first Impressionists and friend of Mary's, had a show at Durand-Ruel at the same time. Pisarro, long since recognized as one of the great French pioneers of the modern idiom, was not selling. His show did not help his financial difficulties.[26]

Mary's show came off well, if not spectacularly. She gained confidence. Lack of money was not her problem, and she did sell her paintings at this time with enough regularity that she could live as she wished. In Paris she was gaining recognition. In America she was almost unknown.

More things continued to happen in Mary Cassatt's career. The Japanese print show of 1890 influenced her work from then on. Seeing how well Degas could draw, she devoted herself to the human figure, spending more long nights on etchings where the slightest error could spoil the whole work. Yet she developed her own way, her own approach to art, her own subject material to produce a series which today are regarded as masterpieces. That she was a woman painter no longer mattered. Her work stood for itself.

Her strength came out in her paintings and prints. For her subjects, she turned to a great extent towards mothers and children: painting after painting of women and their care of their young ones. Perhaps, as a woman herself who gave her life to art, she found her truest success in painting from others what she never experienced—love of a woman for her child.

No one can say how she really felt. Here is perhaps the true reason why so few women become great artists. Instead of following a woman's instinct to produce and love children, she had given up everything to art. But, more than any other subject, she portrayed motherhood in its most intimate and sympathetic form. This she did with a skill that outreached most of her contemporaries turning any subject into art.

After her first one-man show, another opportunity came Mary's way. The great World's Fair of Chicago was being planned. One building was to be known as the Woman's Building and only women were concerned in it. The architect was a young woman, and women painters were commissioned to do murals for the walls. Mrs. Potter Palmer, a woman of great energy from Chicago, was a force behind the whole Exposition, and she was the one to champion Mary Cassatt for a commission to do a mural to be mounted high up in the arches of the building. "Modern Women" was Mary's theme, and she did the painting in the then most modern manner of bright colors, gay, light, and festive.[26] Her mural was lost when the building came down after the Fair was over, but perhaps that was for the best. According to the critics, this work was not up to her standards, and Mary was better able to do the normal oils and prints on which her reputation was being so firmly built.[26]

Another one-man exhibition in Paris followed, this time a large one with many of her oils, pastels and prints. By now Mary Cassatt had reached real fame, spreading out beyond France and touching America. Yet some years later, in 1898, she returned on a trip to Philadelphia, her own city. One of the newspapers carried a social note:

> *Mary Cassatt, sister of Mr. Cassatt, president of the Pennsylvania Railroad, returned from Europe yesterday. She has been studying painting in France and owns the smallest Pekingese dog in the world.*

Such was Philadelphia's recognition of the homecoming of one who was then considered one of the great living painters.

She stayed in America about a year, in Philadelphia visiting family, in Boston doing portraits of children on commission, in

* Philadelphia *Ledger*.[26]

Connecticut again doing commissioned portraits, and then she returned to France.

Mary Cassatt had many American friends, a number of them people of substantial wealth. These she urged to buy French paintings when they came to Paris, and she was responsible for many of the Impressionist paintings being carried back to the United States.

Her sense of knowing what painting was good and what was not gave Mary Cassatt another kind of place in American art. Special friends were Mr. and Mrs. Henry Havemeyer of New York, who were among the few first American collectors of art. Mary Cassatt met Louisine Havemeyer when Louisine was fifteen at boarding school in Paris, and Miss Cassatt herself was twenty-nine. Even then Louisine was interested in paintings. Mary Cassatt showed her the Paris galleries, and together they saw in a window a Degas pastel, called "La Répétition de Ballet." This was the picture of the old ballet master rehearsing his students, which is now so well known. Louisine Elder—her name before she was married—bought it for about one hundred dollars, all the money she had from her allowance. It was her first art purchase, and the beginning of the Havemeyer Collection. It is said that Louisine Havemeyer's grandson sold that pastel in New York in 1965 for $410,000.*

When Louisine, ten years later, married Havemeyer, the two had a joint interest in art. They continued buying, most frequently in Paris with the advice of Mary Cassatt, until the Havemeyer Collection became one of the finest in America.

A fascinating collecting trip was when the Havemeyers and Mary Cassatt went through Italy and then on to Spain buying paintings. They found Veronese pictures in Rome, other Italian classic works elsewhere, and in Spain discovered El Greco. Even as late as 1901, El Greco was not well known except to the art specialists. Mary Cassatt found one of his pictures in an old shop and helped Mrs. Havemeyer buy it for two hundred and fifty dollars. There were more. El Greco's tremendous "View of Toledo" in New York's Metropolitan Museum of Art was a result of that trip. So was a Goya "Portrait of Wellington" now in the National Gallery of Art, Washington, and another El Greco in the Metropolitan, "Cardinal Nino de Guevara."

* *Miss Mary Cassatt,* Frederick A. Sweet, p. 29.

All her life Mary Cassatt spurred her friends and her family into buying art which her own instinct knew to be of timeless quality. That through her influence so many great paintings came across the Atlantic is one more aspect of her genius for which American museums and American people can always be grateful.

MARY CASSATT's later years were marked with frustration and tragic circumstances. Her eyes developed cataracts, and, in spite of numerous operations, for long years she was unable to carry on her painting and drawing. Her friend Degas died, and she made a special effort to be at his funeral in Paris. Others died, too, and she felt alone. World War I swept over France, and she had to leave her beloved villa because it was so close to the front. The results of the war, the changing times, the effects of her blindness, turned the strong character of Mary Cassatt into bitterness and anger.

She died on June 14, 1926, in her French chateau, Beaufresne, at the age of eighty-two. She is buried in the vault of the village cemetery where the others of her family lie with her.[26]

Her life was over, but the work she accomplished in art leaves a heritage to Americans for all time. No matter that she was a woman. She was a very great painter.

PERHAPS the best way to appraise the art of Mary Cassatt is to repeat several stories which simply illustrate the uncompromising nature of her own personality.

In 1904 she was awarded a prize of three hundred dollars by the Pennsylvania Academy of the Fine Arts at its 73rd Annual Exhibition. She refused it. She was grateful though, and did not want to be misunderstood. "I, however," she wrote to the director, "who belong to the founders of the Independent Exhibition must stick to my principles, our principles, which were, no jury, no medals, no awards. Our first exhibition was held in 1879 * and was a protest against official exhibitions and not a grouping of artists with the same art tendencies. We have been since dubbed 'Impressionists' a name which might apply to Monet but can have no meaning when attached to Degas' name. Liberty is the first good in this world and to escape the

* Actually the 4th Impressionist show, but the first in which Mary participated.

83

tyranny of a jury is worth fighting for; surely no profession is so enslaved as ours." [9] She rejected another prize membership in the National Academy of Design in New York. So uncompromising was she with her principles. [26]

Only in 1914 did she accept for herself the Gold Medal of Honor awarded by the Pennsylvania Academy, her one-time school. This was no compromise, for money was not included, and the award was not to a painting but to her as an artist.

What brought fame and lasting recognition to Mary Cassatt, even in her own America which so long ignored her? Her first attribute was absolute sincerity, as the stories told above will show. A second was hard, patient work. A third was a highly developed knowledge of being able to judge a painting.

Sincerity was part of Mary's nature. She said what she thought, even bluntly at times. She might offend or anger people, but she always had their respect. Her sincerity showed through all her work—a sincerity of purpose which permitted no compromise with the best she could do, a sincerity of character which stamped itself into every canvas, every print and drawing.

She had seen at the early beginning of her real training from the paintings of Italian masters on museum walls, that the art which lived on and was vital to later generations reflected the times in which the artists lived. Correggio in Parma was among the first. She lived with his paintings for eight months, copying them and studying them. These were paintings of people, men, women and children, who moved around Correggio as part of his life. What matter that Correggio (1494–1531) lived nearly four hundred years before? His work carried on, timeless.

The same was true of Rubens, whom she discovered in Spain. The Prado Museum in Madrid is full of Flemish and Dutch paintings, all carried down by the Spanish conquerors of the Lowlands in the time of the Inquisition and never returned. What matter that Rubens went back over two hundred and fifty years (1577–1640), less by a century than Correggio? His work had the same vitality of his own contemporary time, and Mary had sense enough to understand it. Those of whatever era who reached back behind them and tried to maintain the past were lifeless, gone and mostly forgotten.

84

This experience of Mary Cassatt is one that artists today try to share. Any painter now seeks to find the essence of his present world, a frightening task in the midst of the fleeting fashions of contemporary art in this our own era. Was it easier in Mary Cassatt's time? Perhaps, but perhaps not considering the difficulties of the first Impressionists.

Cassatt was influenced by many more than those two early classic artists. They happened to be the ones who impressed her most, and who evoked in her the greatest response until she saw the work of Degas. In him, she recognized a new, great classic painter of the same caliber, with the same intentions of using his own time and life around him as his theme. The only difference was that Degas was very much alive, and fighting for his own means of expression and recognition. Degas touched the spark to the dormant bonfire already built in Mary Cassatt's spirit.

The Impressionists, all of them in one way or another,* had rejected the falsity of using only the past. They adopted the present, taking the themes around them and creating their own new styles. Their ways were what Mary wanted. They did what she had already learned was the uphill path to succeeding.

If one looks at a group of Impressionist painters, especially the ones at the height of their careers as a group, it is easy to see a common thread that bound them together. One can find in Mary Cassatt traces not only of Degas, but of Renoir, Pissarro, and Manet. Paul Gauguin was about Mary's age, but he started late and was late enough to be called a post-Impressionist. Yet there is in Gauguin's paintings the same feeling that caught Mary. His subject matter was far different, but the basic forms, composition, and heart of art is remarkably similar.

In subject, Mary Cassatt followed generalities up to a point in her career: toreadors in Spain, portraits of her sister—"A Cup of Tea" (1880: Museum of Fine Arts, Boston). Degas was doing horse races, and then ballet dancers—more and more ballet dancers. Mary found her theme, influenced only by herself: motherhood and children. On this subject she found an inexhaustible inspiration. "Woman and Child Driving" (1880: Philadelphia Museum of Art) was among the first. "Girl Arranging Her Hair" (1886: National Gallery of Art, Washington, D.C.) is a beautiful rendering of youth. "Mother and Child" (1890: Wich-

---

* See previous section: "Berthe Morisot."

ita Art Museum, Wichita, Kansas) was followed by a succession of paintings of motherhood and close family scenes.

How could she avoid being sentimental with such sentimental subjects? Anyone else might have slipped into sticky sweetness. Not Mary Cassatt. Her own forceful personality came through into her work, and she produced masterpieces one after another, each with its own strength.

She learned early from the Impressionists the use of light transformed to color. She placed this new knowledge with what she had already gained from her early studies of classic masters. Especially, she used unerringly her self-taught and self-disciplined skill in drawing. Her figures come alive.

Probably the chief element that makes a work of art is its composition—the planning of forms, lines, and color so that the picture makes a positive statement. Knowledge of composition for its boldest and most effective use is one of the elusive qualities in art. Mary Cassatt knew it as well as anybody.

Influence of the composition of the French painters contemporary with her in Paris shows in many of her works. In the lines of wallpaper, the designs of fabrics in clothing and furniture, the careful placing of counterpoints to circular forms reflect Renoir, Manet and those of the group who revived the art of painting for the sake of the painting itself instead of merely reproducing a subject. At first, Mary Cassatt did not make innovations in composition. She used effectively; in her own way, what others were doing.

After she saw the Japanese prints in 1890, she changed her outlook. If the paintings of Degas and the Impressionists had first opened another world to her, the Japanese simplicity of design in line and color opened a second one. She frankly took over the new viewpoint, and in her own right became one of the leading innovators in compositions.

For a long time she had been doing graphic prints, fine line pictures on metal plates to improve her drawing skill. Now the Japanese influence came into her graphic work as well as her oil paintings and pastels.

Mary found a personal art of color printing, not in the way the Japanese did it but in a manner she worked out for herself. She made an outline of her drawing on a copper plate in a technique called "dry point etching." This is an etching on the metal plate using a special etching needle, which gives a soft and variable line in the final print. Then she "transferred" the drawing to one or two other plates, depending on the number of colors she planned (usually a transfer is made by a method using heavy tracing paper) so that each of the plates corresponded exactly to the original drawing.

Then she took a method already known as "aquatint," a way of making a number of prints in color. She filled in each of the two or three plates she was using with a "ground" where a color was to be printed. A ground in aquatint is powdered rosin, a dry, hard residue from turpentine production. The rosin is sprinkled on the surface to be colored, heated slightly, then it adheres to the plate as a hard granular surface. This is painted over in printer's ink and printed on each copy of the final print by a hand press. A second color is added by another plate, and a third if desired by still another. The original line drawing is done in black or colored ink on one of the separate plates. The result must be a print that satisfies the artist for carrying out his original intention.

This is a difficult process, requiring experience and practice. The amount of ground rosin for each color plate must be controlled, because of the texture wanted in every color area. Each print must be watched for variation, in order that the whole number will conform.

The arts of graphic prints range from engravings and etchings centuries old, to the newest, most sophisticated lithography and silk-screen printings. Fine arts prints, done by the artist or under his control, have nothing to do with commercial prints, however good or bad, which are merely reproductions. Ordinarily, an artist doing prints restricts the number to anything from twenty-five up to several hundred, signs and numbers each print in order, and then destroys the plates so that the series is ended. A custom of fine artists is always to sign and number each print on the margin in pencil, not in ink.

Graphic printing in the fine arts went out of fashion for a time, even after Mary Cassatt's era. Recently, however, it has come back again with innumerable variations. It is frequent now that leading artists make series of prints, which the public can buy at prices far lower than oil paintings or watercolors and yet be assured of a numbered "original." The buying public in general knows little of the difference between "aquatint" and "lithography," between "dry point etchings" and standard etchings.

Understanding of these separate techniques is worthwhile. For an upcoming artist it is essential.

Perhaps the highest point of Mary Cassatt's career was the series of ten aquatint prints done early in the 1890's to match the skill of the Japanese. They were superb. Pissarro said of them, ". . . the result is admirable, as beautiful as Japanese work, and it's done with printer's ink!" [26] These, and following prints, have been known and respected from that time until today, and add greatly to Miss Cassatt's renown.

Mary Cassatt, the young Philadelphia socialite who as a young girl turned against the conventional thing to do, had become one of America's great assets in the fine arts. Not only are her oil paintings, pastels and prints in the leading museums and private collections, but she was one who drew the new glory of French painting in her time to American shores. Through her, and her influence on the Havemeyer Collection, now mostly in the Metropolitan Museum of Art in New York, innumerable works of European art are in the United States which never would have been otherwise. Her influence, through her own great masterpieces as well as what she saw in the genius of others, left a profound stamp on the history of art in the United States.

The finest tribute that could be given to Mary Cassatt was that so many great French artists of her time in Paris considered her their equal, even though she was a woman.

ANALYSIS OF
REPRODUCED
WORK

COLOR PLATE 3 reproduces an oil painting by Mary Cassatt titled "The Boating Party." This painting, oddly for this selection, does not that truly represent Mary Cassatt's work. Yes, it does show a mother and her child sitting at one end of the boat. But most of her paintings, always of human figures, were done in interior settings or in gardens.

"The Boating Party," however, has a special relevancy to Mary Cassatt's career and to her life in Paris. One might for a moment compare this painting of three people in a boat on the water with another of a single rower in a racing shell on the Schuylkill River in Philadelphia, done by her former classmate at the Pennsylvania Academy of the Fine Arts, Thomas Eakins. Without attempting to evaluate one against the other, how different can painters be!

It happened that in 1879 Edouard Manet put as one of his paintings in the Impressionist Exhibition of that year a picture called "In the Boat." Manet's painting was scorned by the critics and public, and was rejected by everyone after the show. Yet Mary loved the painting, and finally had the opportunity to urge her friend Mrs. Havemeyer to buy it. This painting by Manet is now in the Metropolitan Museum of Art, part of the Havemeyer Collection.

Mary had always admired Manet, twelve years older than she was, and who died young, at the age of fifty-one, in 1883. Ten years later, in 1893, she finished her own painting of "The Boating Party," in which there is a strong feeling of affinity with Manet's "In the Boat," shown for the first time four years before he died. The content of the paintings is different, but the subject and the spirit suggest that through all these years Mary Cassatt kept Manet's work in mind, and finally gave her own rendition of it. It seems to be more than coincidental.

Technically, this painting is almost flawless. In composition, one's eye is caught first by the strong white curve of the boat's gunwale pushing up and in toward the central point of the child in the woman's lap. The push to the viewer's eye is aided by the almost corresponding curve of the under line of the sail, and by the forward movement of the oar. Yet the long, long line of the boat's gunwale is broken for a moment by the oarlock and oar, so that, although serving its purpose, it is not over-accented. Then, basically, that strong, fast push of the eye on the left side of the picture toward the child is balanced by the great dark bulk of the oarsman on the right. Even the inclination of the oarsman's body, toward the child, makes a kind of hidden semi-circular form toward the main focal point. The rower's dark figure is broken by the blue waistband, and the seat on which he is sitting forms a base to the composition and adds reality to the boat.

Once again, the horizontal seat of the boat is offset by the narrow distant shoreline, not too predominant because it is broken by the top of the oarsman's hat. The shoreline is stopped, too, by the sail, which in an indirect way seems to curve around out of sight to hold the whole picture in place.

Even the circular shape of the man's hat seems to push the eye down, and this secondary push is picked up by the boy's hat, swinging the viewer's eye further down on the child. Both curves are abetted by the woman's hat. Yet the child himself, while the ultimate focal point, is not everything in the picture. Once the eye rests upon him, gaze is diverted away to the rest of the painting because the child's face is somewhat obscured.

Note especially how the line holding the sail to the stern of the boat also holds the picture together. Visualize the painting handled any other way.

None of these things pointed out are accidental. They are done by plan and partly by intuition. These are the threads which make great paintings.

An earlier painting, "Child in a Straw Hat," done around 1886 (Color Plate 4), shows an entirely different side of Mary Cassatt. In this picture, which seems so deceptively simple, all background composition is eliminated except the purity of color itself. The little girl could have been standing before a wall, but even if so the wall has yielded any literal quality to beautiful color gradations that supplement—or, better, implement the colors of the figure.

This painting of a nameless child implies a mood. Out of that mood flows a very definite personality. The girl is petulant, impatient, probably wondering why on earth she has to stand so still just to have her likeness put onto a piece of canvas. Because Mary Cassatt could catch that mood, her painting comes to life vibrantly. One cannot help but feel sympathetic warmth toward the barely tolerant little girl.

Here is a suggestion of the influence of Degas, and surely a trace of the artist's familiarity with Renoir. Yet as a work of art it is pure Cassatt, only casually built on external techniques. If anything, it may reflect back to the impact of Rubens, brought up to date with Impressionist color.

Close and lingering study of this painting reveals more of its secrets. The drawing not only captures the child's personality, but is a superb example of the definition of form. The roundness of the neck, the fullness of the arms give substance to the body, as do the shoulders. The hat is too big, and probably is not the child's at all. Someone seems to have plunked a woman's hat— her mother's? Mary's own?—on top of the head. Yet the hat adds everything to the child's character, as well as to the composition of the painting.

Notice the eyes. They are not quite alike, and not quite in line with each other. In life, eyes are frequently different in size or formation, just as one side of the human face ordinarily has some variation from the other. The discerning artist sees these slight differences and turns them to advantage in heightening character and reality. So Mary Cassatt did with this child, for it is the eyes which are most expressive. The slight tilt of the head, the downward pull of one corner of the mouth help to emphasize a pouting disapproval.

Then, in seeing the painting more and more clearly, the way Mary Cassatt used counter-balancing arcs in her composition stands out clearly. The top of the hat and the forward rim are downward arcs; they are balanced in turn by the upward circles of the back of the hat, of the chin, and of the pinafore collar. The result neatly contains the face as the clear focal point of the painting. The composition holds the arcs, however, through their repetition in the shoulders of the pinafore and sleeves of the blouse, once more offset by the upturning arc of the arms. The latter goes so far as to offset the hat, too.

The result is a portrait of pleasure to look at and feel. So easily painted? It is a masterpiece of skill and knowledge beneath its simplicity.

On the other hand, the dry point and aquatint prints which Mary Cassatt made after seeing the Paris exhibition of Japanese art in 1890, reveal a very different approach and style. Cassatt explored the deepest complexities of design and composition. Her set of ten "Japanese" prints became famous almost immediately after she did them.

In these prints Mary Cassatt brought together into one area the knowledge and experience of three major sources: first, the beautiful quality of line and composition of Oriental art; second, the rhythm of pattern and color which mark the work of her contemporary Impressionists; and especially, her own skill and knowledge gained from her long studies of the great European master painters. Perhaps she was the first one ever to succeed in such a monumental effort.

Two of these Japanese-inspired prints are reproduced here. One, "La Toilette" (Plate 12), shows a girl washing her hands and face in a basin, with a pitcher standing on the floor beside her. The other, "Coiffure" (Plate 13), is of a seated girl arranging her hair in front of a mirror. Of such prosaic subjects, Mary Cassatt created masterpieces of drawing and composition.

The process of making prints by combining dry point etching and aquatint coloring has already been described. In both these prints one sees clearly how she used the simplicity of Oriental style lines to define the figures of the girls and the furniture. Both girls have their clothing around their waists. Notice with

91

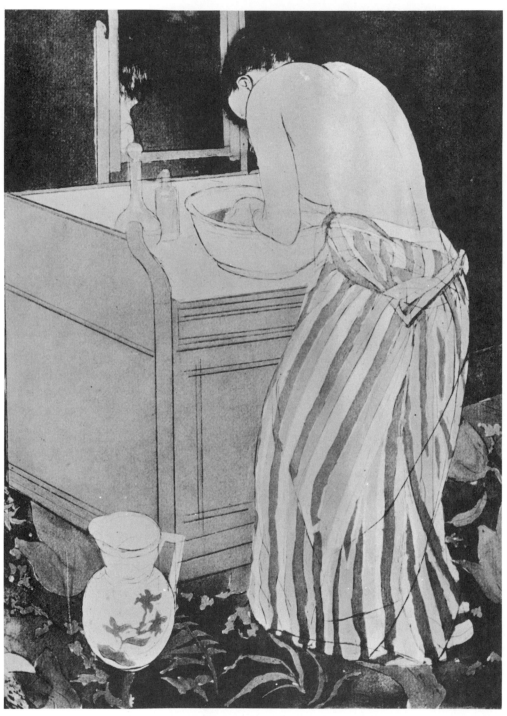

PLATE 12

La Toilette, by Mary Cassatt.
Courtesy of The Brooklyn Museum.

Coiffure, by Mary Cassatt.
Courtesy of The Brooklyn Museum.

PLATE 13

93

how few lines the painter has shown their bodies, heads and arms. The forms are rounded and full, the limbs forward and backward in motion. Only superb craftsmen of drawing can do so much with such economy of line. The back and the arm of the girl leaning over the washbasin is a prime example of the perfection drawing can achieve. The basin itself and the bottles contain lines which are not only true, but expressive. They become more than just lines, but the objects themselves. The commode on which the basin rests, and the frame of the mirror in the second print, are drawn with exactness, where the slightest mistake in using the sharp tool on the metal plate could have spoiled the picture.

Beyond the drawing, Mary Cassatt incorporated patterns into the prints which complement the simple figure drawing. In the first print the stripes of the full-length dress are balanced by the floral designs of the carpet picked up discreetly on the side of the water pitcher. The designs of the dress and the carpet counter the plain severity of the piece of furniture. These balances of strength of patterns and forms were typically Impressionist—a style not long afterward used by Matisse for his own art.

The second print shows the same intentions. This time the chair cover is striped more broadly, and the carpet pattern—a different one—is held by the larger but more subtle design of the wallpaper. The reflections of all of these in the mirror complete the whole composition. Once again there is the strong use of designs to offset the simple quality of the figure—so simple that even the clothing of the girl is indicated by only a few lines to reveal the idea of the thighs and legs beneath.

Of all her work, it might be safe to say that Mary Cassatt's prints proved best her individuality, skill, experience and painstaking care in creating fine art.

THE
PORTRAIT BY
DEGAS

ABOUT 1884, some nine years after he first met her, Mary Cassatt's great and good friend Edgar Degas painted her portrait. It was not the first time he had done so or probably the last, for Mary often posed for him when he was doing costumed figures.

This particular portrait (Plate 11), however, seems different in intent. As in the previous comment on Manet, this book makes no attempt to analyze a painting by Edgar Degas. Yet there is something so wonderful about this portrait that a remark about it comes spontaneously.

As one looks at Mary Cassatt's face, a feeling comes through of the deep and lasting friendship between the two painters. Though the pose is informal, the interpretation which Degas has given to her pensive and faraway expression as she holds what seem to be photographs reveals the depth of his respect and admiration. She herself, even from the canvas, communicates so much of her own personality. The painting gives an increasing sense of the understanding each for the other as no words could.

PLATE 14

Self-portrait, by Cecilia Beaux.
National Academy of Design, New York.

CHAPTER 6

Cecilia Beaux

1863–194?

NOT every artist must be a pioneer, and break into new fields. Monroe Wheeler, for years an instigator of spectacular shows of international contemporary art at the Museum of Modern Art in New York, once defined contemporary art as "saying something new, or something old in a new way." This is actually true, in the case of any artist who wishes to be a part of the forward movement in the long-continuous and advancing history of art. The hundreds who dare the unknown and unaccepted, who fail—and the few who dare and succeed—move art ahead. They are the ones who anticipate what is coming in ways and customs of life, and who could win a reluctant public to change.

But what about artists who are content to use what exists, and to build their reputations on their own contemporary ideals? There are innumerable ones who do, without the drive to forge into untried areas, and usually they earn less respect in the final analysis or are completely forgotten. They are the ones who say "something old in an old way." Only a master artist can have the technical skill, the discernment to avoid clichés, and the wisdom to overcome the handicap of repeating what has gone before. *Current* success is more likely, but respect in the long run is apt to wear out with passing time.

One who overcame these obstacles, and yet never ran the risks of venturing into radical and untrod paths of the future was an American woman, best known for her startlingly real portraits

CHILDHOOD, AND THE BEGINNING

97

which have recorded the personalities of great people in a way distinctly her own. Cecilia Beaux did not change the art of her time, or blaze future trails. She used what was accepted in current art, and built her fame on that. Her skill, intuition, and sound judgment did the rest. As a painter, Cecilia Beaux has been recognized internationally.

She was born in Philadelphia, and remained a true Philadelphian all her life although she lived and studied abroad and spent much time in New York and in Massachusetts. She was gentle, conservative, and felt the beauty—a suspect word today—of things around her.

Cecilia's personality which shone in her work developed in her childhood—or, perhaps, her childhood was influenced by an inherited personality and by her surroundings. At any rate, she remembered vividly happenings when she was very young: things which affected always her sense of "seeing" and understanding the visual beauties of the natural world. When she fell into a kitchen well and almost drowned, her family thought of the near tragedy. Cecilia remembered only the square of light above her, and the "black and gold motion" of the water. She wrote of this in her autobiography,[34] and also of a time when she was alone with her aunt by the side of a lazy Pennsylvania stream in summertime. No one could ever tell this story as descriptively as Cecilia herself. She was at the time only six, but her recollection in later years described the creek and bridge below the farmhouse where she spent the summer, and:

"But in all this there is only one very vivid recollection. Perhaps, for a wonder, I was alone with the aunt who always had her sketchbook and pencil with her. Strangely enough, though the scene before me was to bewitch memory for a lifetime, I had no wish to draw it.

"Looking up the stream, the little river was quiet, almost noiseless, and, unusual in an American landscape, its banks and stretches, as far as one could see, were lawns of vivid green; a grassy pasture, kept close by grazing creatures of the farm. Great trees, without undergrowth, threw broad delicious shadows, between which long shafts of summer sunshine lay upon the grass, and down the greensward walked solemnly a long line of snowy geese, bending necks here and there, spreading wings, or lowering yellow bills to taste the grass. From shadow, through streams of light, they came. It was my first conscious perception of the beauty of white plumage moving in a setting which had the undisturbed perfection of a classic pastoral. I knew nothing, probably thought nothing; I am sure said nothing; I was nought but an unsullied page that was constituted to hold unfaded the scene impressed upon it by the same hand that made the image. . . .

"Perhaps the stability of memory is always due to the influence of atavism upon the subconscious mind. What we have come from—which is what we fundamentally are—revives suddenly, under the stimulus of a remote, germinal, ancestral urge, recognized and desired as it appears unsummoned in the unlike present; and so it passes into the crucible of performing energy, as the closest, strongest ally of creative impulse; in fact, the guardian and inspirer of our *Taste*. Taste that in its indomitable demand has nothing in common with the ready-made whimsicality dictated by weariness and satiety.

"The aunt, doubtless thinking of her unfinished sketch and her vagarious niece, trudged up the dusty hill to the farmhouse, the noisy family, and dinner, neither of them aware that anything had happened during their quiet morning. The child (Cecilia herself), perhaps lagged behind to pick and peel a mullen pod, and had to be called and hurried on. She hated the dusty road that burned her feet, hated the roadside dust on leaf and fern. At all events the fecund morning passed unnoticed. Well it is that most really important matters are unobserved at their advent, that no ticker-tape is thrown upon the breeze, nor are reporters present, when a seed falls into a furrow that will bear the richest corn in the crop, or the small hard vessel drops to earth with the grandest of oaks in its vitals." [34]

Cecilia Beaux wrote, in later years, with almost total recall of that childhood morning which meant so much to her later.

Cecilia's mother died when she was only twelve days old, and her heartbroken father was left with the baby. Her grandmother —her mother's mother—took charge, and in company with Cecilia's two aunts, brought her up. They were all a family with New England background, although her own father was French. Philadelphia had become their home, and it was Philadelphia where Cecilia spent her childhood, and, indeed, much of her younger life. Her childhood was happy, uneventful, and very much that of a genteel young girl.

Yet her youthful days were already becoming filled with ex-

99

periences of things and people, and events. Her memories were not in any established order of time. Things happened, and Cecilia, the child, remembered them. Later, as a grown-up, she did not recall specific emotions about those things that happened in her early days. As she wrote in her autobiography, young children do not remember emotions as much as facts or events. The fact remembered creates the later emotion.

A visit to the museum of the Pennsylvania Academy of the Fine Arts left this kind of memory. Cecilia was taken there at a very young age. The Academy then was in an earlier building, before its location at Broad and Cherry Streets, and Cecilia remembered it as a "dark old building," quite far downtown. While her aunts went through the galleries, young Cecilia was absorbed by the sight of a huge painting hanging over a staircase. From the gallery a balustrade hid a clear view of the painting for a child of her height. So Cecilia lay with her head on the floor, from which point she could clearly see, under the balustrade, the rushing horses, the people falling beneath the hoofs, the prostrate ones on the ground: the dramatic scene of "Death on a Pale Horse," by Benjamin West.* She was more curious than impressed. She knew the Revelations, and what the painting illustrated; the name of the artist, his fame, or the fact of this being a work of art did not interest her. She simply gazed at the scene until she was found and put back on her feet.[34]

She was older when she was taken to see a private collection of paintings owned by the Gibson family in Philadelphia. Millet's "Angelus" was in the collection, and on first sight of it, the painting made a peculiar impression on the still young Cecilia. How could two people facing each other say their prayers publicly in a field? The "purple-grey and black" tones did not impress her as did the brighter colors of other paintings in the collection. Yet the foreign and new world of French peasants struck her as something that she would some day know.† Cecilia's favorite was a portrait of a young man by a French painter, Couture, who was then quite an old man. The portrait had a form and line which she seemed to understand only instinctively. She remem-

* Now permanently installed in the front galleries of the Pennsylvania Academy of the Fine Arts, Philadelphia.

† Mr. William Gibson, the original buyer and owner of most of this Philadelphia collection was later persuaded to exchange the "Angelus" for another Millet painting, for the reason that the

bered, too, Courbet's landscape of a tree standing alone against a grayish background. A "Birth of Venus" by Cabanel was not "one of (her) friends among the pictures." "Turquoise and cream," she called the romantic nude, and it evoked only the response to bright color. A small Boldini made her think most. Its subject was a girl walking under a French summer sky, introducing clouds, trees, and landscape entirely unfamiliar to a young girl raised in Philadelphia.

"How could I dream of being an artist?" Cecilia wrote in her autobiography. "I never did. I was too much occupied, and I did not see 'myself' as having any possible relation or participation in what I saw around me."

She saw around her in the fabulous Gibson house not only the collection of "modern" (her quotes) French paintings, but also a conservatory which brought summer into a cold, gray day of winter outdoors. Great ferns, flowers, dampness of earth and bird songs made a background to the paintings, both never to be forgotten by an impressionable child.[34]

CECILIA BEAUX never attended school until she was fourteen. At that time, shortly after the end of the Civil War, this was not unusual. Geography, arithmetic and reading were taught by her aunts under the keen eye of her grandmother. She learned sewing, and made a desperate and quite helpless effort toward music.

EARLY
MATURITY

But at fourteen she was sent to the most fashionable girls' school in Philadelphia. It was run—not only run, but owned, operated and ruled—by Miss Lyman, one of the extinct headmistresses who used to educate girls into being young ladies. Cecilia Beaux herself would surely agree to the unhappy fact that today there are no more iron-handed school mistresses who give their students more through their own personalities than through studies taught by their staffs. Yet Cecilia took a far different view of her school than Miss Lyman ever suspected. To Cecilia, the place was a fascinating stage filled with interplay of characters, with people of varying personalities, of a range of life to which she had never been exposed.

> former was not that good as a painting. It is now in the Louvre, one of the world's most reproduced pictures. The greater part of the Gibson Collection was finally bequeathed to the Pennsylvania Academy of the Fine Arts, including Courbet's "Tree," where it now remains.

Miss Lyman's School had certain enviable characteristics which we would now call ultramodern. There were no grades. There were no examinations. Not too long ago these features would be called innovations, but Miss Lyman flourished ninety years ago. Each girl was placed in the particular course where her previous experience seemed to put her, regardless of age. So Cecilia took beginning Latin with younger girls, and French and English composition with classes far older. American history was on a par with her own age. Every girl, regardless of wealth or social background, wore plain woolen dresses, often homemade. Black or white stockings, with low-heeled shoes and aprons were school attire.

The true discipline of Miss Lyman's was a monthly report sent to parents. Unfortunately, Cecilia's were not very good. She was more interested in personalities at the school itself than in her studies. Her one great triumph was to be promoted from the English composition class of her own age group to the highest level because of her writing ability.

A sidelight of Miss Lyman's to Cecilia was the fact that drawing classes were held in an upstairs room of the school. She never joined in them. What she saw of the students' work as they came downstairs revolted her. She said in her later writing that the endless, smudged charcoal drawings were her introduction to the kind of thing she was destined to know so well in later life in selecting students for the Pennsylvania Academy of the Fine Arts. She would not have been dragged to those classes at school.

Cecilia went to Miss Lyman's for only two years, but they were an unforgettable time of her life—even to remembering that girls were told never to glance across the street to the windows of the Philadelphia Club where, behind the shining glass, "mischievous old gentlemen might have ogled them from over their newspapers." [34] Whether any girls did look, Cecilia did not say. Surely the old gentlemen, fathers, uncles, grandfathers of socialite girls themselves, would never have said either.

Then Cecilia Beaux reached the end of true childhood and early maturity, a time of observing naturally light, colors, sounds, things and people. She wrote later a memorable thought which deserves to be quoted now:

> *"Oh, educators and child analysts, see that you do not handle the delicate fibres of young consciousness and perception until the antennae are limp and powerless to*

feel. Do not maul them, or, gorging them with your experimental diet, deprive them of all appetite, their supreme prerogative and birth-right as developing creatures. Do not rob the maturity or age of these children. Give them a chance. . . ." [34]

AT HOME, Cecilia's family thought that she had shown enough interest and skill in out-of-school drawing lessons to warrant regular art instruction. Still, she did not have any idea of being an artist. "The gulf between me and such an ambition was too great." She knew nothing about colors, canvas, paints. When she thought of the Gibson Collection paintings, they were far from stirring her personally. She said she had never heard of "self-expressionism." To her life itself was to be enjoyed. She did enjoy everything around her, houses, furnishings, clothing, above all, people.

Her uncle must have known through a second sense that his young niece had an inclination toward art, as yet unfelt. So cautiously he approached the idea. He had a relative, Miss Katherine Drinker, who was an artist and had a studio in downtown Philadelphia. If her uncle was reluctant to have Cecilia face an outside world, this was a safe opportunity. He arranged that Cecilia become a pupil of Miss Drinker.*

Here was young Cecilia's first introduction to a real studio, and she loved its mystery and the light that came through the skylight. She was set to work copying lithographs with a Conté crayon, using line with the strictest discipline. She worked hard, and her teacher approved, but Cecilia could not be satisfied with the hard lines she produced on a glaring yellow paper. The results were frustrating. After a year an art school opened in Philadelphia, run by a young Dutchman. Her uncle investigated the school first, found it proper, and sent Cecilia there.

The Dutch instructor first made her do an enlarged drawing of a head from a small lithograph. She was used to copying, but to make such an enlargement terrified her. She did it so well that one was enough.

Other students were drawing from plaster casts of sculpture, and Cecilia envied them. Her instructor instead arranged a series

---

* Katherine Drinker later became Mrs. Thomas Jenner, and her brother, Henry Drinker, married Cecilia's sister Aimée. The Drinker Collection of Cecilia Beaux' paintings was one of the best.

of dust-covered, gray plaster geometric forms: blocks, spheres, circular columns. They were mechanically made, offered no incentive. The teacher explained little to Cecilia. As she worked on her drawing, she suddenly found understanding of light and shading, the use of cast shadows, subtleties of line and tones to define form. She discovered for herself principles of perspective. She never knew whether the Dutch instructor's idea was purely accidental, or whether he had a true perception of the value of his "still-life." It was enough that she gained knowledge that lasted all her life.

Next came drawing from the antique casts, which she had longed to do. The practice was different. The cold plaster yielded nothing of the beauty of the original marble, which in turn was carved from models of living flesh.

It used to be traditional for art students to be forced to draw in painstaking detail of shading from the "antique," before being presented with the problems of a live model. Often this disciplinary enslavement to plaster lasted for months on end, even for one drawing. Undoubtedly the practice did create a technical efficiency in drawing form and shading, but the results were necessarily as lifeless as the casts themselves. Thomas Eakins abolished the necessity for this study from the Pennsylvania Academy's routine, substituting the dissection of human bodies, but after his discharge from the Academy for his modern ideas the cast drawing requirement crept back again. In contemporary art instruction, the method has fortunately all but disappeared, except in some foreign countries.* Now a beginning student in drawing can start at once from the living model.

Cecilia Beaux felt the weight of the antique drawing, and doubted that anything of value survived from it, for herself or for other students. Mary Cassatt, in her student time, felt that she had gained from it.

One day another student brought into school a set of bones of a skeleton. This entranced Cecilia. The bones were unlike natural things—more abstract, although she did not use that word in her description. Their forms gave new and unexpected lines. Their firm color and translucence offered the greatest inspiration. She learned, too, the names of each bone, and certainly it gave her the unerring ability to understand the structure of the head.

* Namely, in some of the art schools in Italy.

Other schools followed, and then one day her uncle took her to visit a commercial lithograph shop. She was greatly interested in the use of stones. The owner of the shop loaned her a stone, and she did a black-and-white drawing on it of an actress from a photograph. It was accepted for an advertisement, the actress was delighted, and Cecilia had done her first commission.

A commission followed to do a series of lithographs of ancient fossils as illustrations for a geological report. The work was concentrated and painstaking in order to bring out the forms of bones from the surrounding matrix of rock. She did so well that more important commissions came to her from the same sources.

Cecilia Beaux might have fallen into a career of illustrations of old skulls, bones and teeth. She rebelled at last. She took a course in china painting, and tried doing children's portraits on fired china. They were instantly successful. Orders came from far away, with photographs, locks of hair of children she had never seen. Even then she was ashamed of this work. It was the lowest depth, she records, that she ever reached in commercial art.

She wanted to attend the School of the Pennsylvania Academy of the Fine Arts. Her uncle intervened. She was good at copying, it was true. Yet there was no reason to think that her interest was serious and lasting. Her Quaker uncle shuddered at the thought of a life class. "Why," said he, "should Cecilia be thrown into what he termed "a rabble of untidy and indiscriminate art students and no one knew what influence?" [34]

Some of the ultimately great names in American art history were studying, or about to study, at the Academy at this time. Henry McCarter, Alexander Sterling Calder (father of Alexander Calder, creator of the "mobile," and son of Alexander Milne Calder who did the William Penn statue on top of Philadelphia's City Hall) and others destined for fame were among them. Thomas Eakins was still on the Academy faculty.

But another opportunity opened for Cecilia, and this one her uncle approved of. A former schoolmate at Miss Lyman's was taking up painting with serious intentions. She rented a studio and established a regular class. Models posed three mornings a week, and a painter named William Sartain agreed to come from New York once every two weeks to give criticism. Cecilia Beaux was asked to join. New life opened for her.

She was later to write of this class: ". . . the record of this adventure, for so it now appears to me, should be written with a pen of fire. . . . It was my first conscious contact with the high and ancient demands of art . . . a new world which was to be continuously mine." [34]

WILLIAM SARTAIN's class lasted two years. Sartain, although not a great painter himself, did make an impression on Philadelphia, particularly on Cecilia Beaux. He himself had been trained in the French Romantic school, and his work carried on the tradition of landscapes, seascapes, and especially heads. In the latter respect, he was a fine teacher, and with each criticism of Cecilia's painting he imparted to her more of what to look for in drawing the model's head, the basic forms as well as the individuality. Accurate proportion made the individual, and he increased Cecilia's perception of mass and structure.

By the end of two years, when Sartain could no longer give time to the class, Cecilia Beaux was ready to launch her own career. She set up a studio, and planned her first full-scale painting.

She created it in her mind: it was to be a portrait of her sister, sitting with her three-year-old son on her lap. She made tentative drawings, and as she thought about it, even the title came to her. It was in French, and she did not want to translate it: "Les derniers jours de l'enfance." [34]

The next problem was to have her sister and small nephew come to the studio to pose. They lived some distance away. The boy had a suit just the color that Cecilia wanted, but her sister's dress had to be improvised. Cecilia loaned her a black jersey dress, and she made one black satin sleeve, with lace, for the arm which would show. A crepe shawl of her grandmother's did well draped as a skirt. She borrowed a family rug, and a small Drinker heirloom table. A small piece of paneling stained like mahogany and moved along as the painting progressed did for a wainscotting between floor and wall. No chair was right, and Cecilia finally invented what she needed to show in the picture.

So the painting was undertaken, and made possible by the enduring patience of her sister and to the amusement of the little boy. A girl who had a studio next door helped by posing for the draped knees and the feet. The painting was finally completed (Plate 15).*

* See further comments in a later section for an analysis of the painting, now owned by Cecilia's great-niece, Mrs. Henry Saltonstall.

PLATE 15

Les Derniers Jours de l'Enfance, by Cecilia Beaux.
Courtesy of Cecilia D. Saltonstall.

"Les derniers jours d'enfance" was exhibited at the Pennsylvania Academy. A friend of Cecilia's, on her way to France, insisted on taking it with her for submission to the Salon in Paris. "The Salon!" To Cecilia, the idea was insane. But the friend took it off the stretcher and rolled it up to carry into her stateroom on the boat. In Paris, it was stretched again, put into a frame, and sent to the jury of the Salon. Cecilia's painting was accepted. This was about the year 1885.

She never learned what the French critics or the public thought of it. When the painting finally came back to her in Philadelphia, it carried French labels and numbers, but the canvas could not tell the story of what had happened, or what comments were expressed.

The experience with her painting confirmed a plan of Cecilia's —that she too should go to Europe. She had saved some money, and her uncle supplied the rest. A cousin was to go with her. They sailed from New York on a wintry day in January, straight into a cold Atlantic storm. Cecilia suffered the agonies of seasickness. But when the ship finally docked at Antwerp and she put foot for the first time on the soil of Europe, she experienced all the thrills and excitement that must come to anyone of receptive mind.

All the new sights and scenes of the waterfront, the rooftops and houses, the people, turned themselves into mental paintings. The first afternoon she saw great works of art by Rubens in the Cathedral at Antwerp. She described herself as being caught in a tidal wave of emotion. Tears blinded her eyes. The blues and the reds, the majesty of the vision, the incredible use of paint pigment to evoke the senses—Cecilia, standing before the greatness of art, was overwhelmed.

These, and the experiences that came one after another so soon afterward, moved an alert mind forward. Cecilia went on to Paris, and there in the Louvre discovered Rembrandt. His "Supper at Emmaus" provided her with new insight. "Again we must say, can this be painting?"

Cecilia and her cousin lived in a pension typically French, without heat and furnished with second-hand things. They did not see the sun in Paris until May, and endured the usual French winter of melting snow, rain and fog. At the same time, Cecilia entered the Académie Julien, an art school famous long before and after for its drawing instruction.

Cecilia Beaux, whose work was already shown at the Paris Salon and had long studied on her own, had a prior belief that she would be far ahead of other students, more advanced and superior. She found out quickly enough that the Académie was a "business enterprise," and could not be maintained for gifted students only. Every nationality was represented among students. She entered the life class, and her first criticism from the instructor was not only successful but opened her eyes to the French method of teaching. This did not use analytic methods of saying what was right and wrong, but was in the higher level of approval or disapproval. Cecilia found herself considered as only one of the group of hard-working students.

Her comments written at this time are of value to *all* art students: "What peace, what space for deliberation, there was *in being a student!* I did not have to think of exhibition, or any of the sordid growths that flourish about student life when permitted, and in fact are planted by their directors in many schools now. It was all between the fascinating object and myself. Not even the master would come between. He would say little. If I felt that my work did not interest him, something was wrong, blind, in it, and I was goaded into greater effort." [34]

She said more about—and to—students. Cecilia eventually became an instructor to students and knew their problems and their doubts. Another American girl from California was a student at Julien's, one who had no familiarity with culture or art and who had little background at all. Her great attribute was only an incredible faculty for drawing. From her rough charcoal came magical interpretations of form and figure, which were acclaimed by the instructors.

Then she disappeared. Cecilia never heard of her again. She spoke of this girl: "She was one of the gifted who have no sense of their own value, so far do their dreams carry them beyond what they do, and discouragement, with such, may submerge effort. So the rarest appears and floats away while the ordinary we have always with us."

But in speaking of art in general she said: "A student in art must never expect regular progress or to 'acquire' systematically. The gods will send him messages from strange places and at unexpected times. Long periods of apparent stagnation will occur, and, after what he has lamented as time lost, 'the fruitful hours of still increase' will find him suddenly in a new elevation." [34]

How true these words are for the impatient student of today,
who so often forgets that he is still a student and not yet a professional. They apply as well for the mature artist who has
dared to persist down the long and rock-filled road of art.

Two years of study in Paris were broken by a trip to Italy—
Venice and Florence—and at the end a visit to friends in England.
The latter led to portrait commissions, and a quick return to
Cambridge.

Afterward, she returned to Philadelphia, and had five years
of truly professional work. Cecilia was growing in reputation, in
skill, and the body of her achievement. She used pastel, learning
from the technique the accurate pre-understanding of color on the
paper, and transferred that knowledge to oil painting on canvas.

Cecilia had friends in Paris, one of whom was an American illustrator and painter, Henry McCarter. McCarter and another
Philadelphian, John Lambert whose studio at home Cecilia was
to use later, persuaded her to send a group of paintings to the
current Salon, named that year the "Champs de Mars." She did
send over five paintings, all of which were accepted, and led immediately to another trip by Cecilia to Paris. This time she wanted
to see her work on the walls. The five pictures were placed together, and were good. Cecilia was upset by one ray of sunshine,
which penetrated the gallery and distracted from the surfaces of
the paintings. McCarter and Lambert laughed at her, and took
her to lunch in the sunshine outdoors. She was forever grateful
to these friends.*

THE
FULL FLOWER
OF
MATURITY

CECILIA BEAUX was destined to grow from that time on, in ability
and in knowledge, in opportunities and friendships. She was in
Philadelphia, and then in New York, and in Boston. She was
received everywhere with admiration, respect, and love for her
nature and intelligence. She quoted in her writing with humor
from a Philadelphia newspaper which said that "Miss Cecilia
Beaux is the best Female Portrait Painter in Philadelphia." The
compliment was meant to be sincere, but in itself it bespoke of

---

* Henry McCarter's name and friendship with Cecilia Beaux must
be brought out in this book for a very personal reason on the part
of one of the authors. "Mac" was Winthrop Neilson's first art instructor and gave so much of the joy and understanding of art
that personal tribute to him is due: "Mac was the finest art
teacher I have known, or know of."—W.N.

a certain quaintness in regard to the female sex which was not entirely Philadelphian, then or later.

Meanwhile, she had been making friendships with the great names of her time, in art and otherwise. John Singer Sargent, the portrait painter whom she admired, was one. Although she did not share their opinion, others felt she excelled Sargent. Friends included Augustus St. Gaudens, the sculptor, Mark Twain, John La Farge, and Winslow Homer. Cecilia Beaux moved among the elite. She did portrait after portrait, drawing after drawing, each of which added to her stature and reputation—"female"or not.

Years passed, and then—with the greatest modesty on Cecilia's own part—she was to do a portrait of Mrs. Theodore Roosevelt, wife of the President of the United States. She went to Washington a number of times to do the work, and the Red Room of the White House was turned over to her for a studio. The painting was intended to be only of the President's wife, but somehow her daughter Ethel crept in, and was painted, too. During the morning poses the President himself would appear, looking, but not making disturbing comments. The White House during Teddy Roosevelt's administration was a lively and noisy place, filled with children, a variety of pets, and especially by the immense and lively personality of the President himself.

She wrote about a dinner at the White House, where Paderewski and his wife were house guests. The great pianist played afterward to a special audience. "By the time he got to the Polonaise—finest of all (at least to me), the one with the tragic octaves as well—I think it may have been better than hearing Chopin himself. All of Paderewski's gigantic power was back of it. I don't believe he has ever gone higher, farther, or deeper. I nearly broke under it. . . ."

Afterward Cecilia was invited to the Roosevelts' home at "Sagamore Hill," Oyster Bay, Long Island. "The President ate two mutton chops for his luncheon," she wrote home. "Not much to keep *it* up on. I sat next to him, so I know." [34] The *it* referred to the man who played tennis all morning and who was apt to spend a whole day paddling a canoe across the waters of Oyster Bay and Long Island Sound.

AFTER World War I, a group of prominent people in the United States commissioned five artists to do three portraits each of leading figures for the allied cause during the war. Cecilia Beaux was chosen to be one of the five. Her subjects: Cardinal Mercier, of Belgium, one of the great heroes of the war; Admiral Lord Beatty, the famous English Navy leader; and Georges Clemenceau, Premier of France.

These portraits were to be presented to the United States Government, as a record in this country of the Europeans with whom American destiny had been linked.

"Great portraits of great people are very rare," Cecilia Beaux said. She approached the commissions given to her with humility, and a great sense of the responsibility. To give posterity any idea of the power of these men through a static material called for "a conscious and just mind, no less than the gods' gift of subconscious force." [34]

Cardinal Mercier was the first subject of Cecilia's new commission. She writes in her book of the experience she had in Belgium in order to portray the man who had stood against German demands during the occupation of Belgium in World War I. Mercier had helped his people through their years of hardship and trials. Cecilia found him an interesting man, of character and strength—a man who knew sorrow and the greatest human responsibilities, who carried even after the war a heavy load of Church work, but who was responsive to her every wish for the portrait. Cecilia lived in a convent while the picture was being done. For two months during the summertime she had the perfect experience of a portrait painter, in interpreting through paint and canvas her expression of a man loved by his people and his country, and respected by the world.

This was only one of the great rewards of a lifetime of work.

Another was carrying out the commission for the portrait of Admiral Sir David Beatty—Lord Beatty, the English hero of the Battle of Jutland in which the Royal British Navy defeated the German fleet. Cecilia did the portrait in London, and found the Admiral one of the most challenging subjects of her career. At first he was reluctant to spare the time or take the trouble to pose for a portrait. He was strong-willed and impatient. "A falcon ready for the chase," Cecilia called him. His nose was broad at the base and fine at the tip, eyebrows bending close in to the nose, gray eyes that had an intense, farseeing look (see Plate 18).

She caught it all, the personality of the Admiral, his strength, the determination even in his hands as they rested on his sword.

The painting of Clemenceau, the "Tiger of France," was different again from any other. This man had brought France, together with the great Allied leaders, through the dark days of 1917 and 1918 up to the Armistice which spelled German defeat. Clemenceau then was the negotiator for France on working out the complications of the Treaty of Versailles.

Here was a man tempestuous, stormy, volatile—another who resented a portrait being done. He gave in to Cecilia's quiet persuasiveness, her tact. He allowed her to come again and again to see him, and slowly she built up the portrait of an elusive, yet blunt personality. She struggled to present a true picture of one of the strongest, most forceful characters of the early twentieth century.

The portraits of the three heroes of World War I are now in the National Collection of Fine Arts, of The Smithsonian Institution in Washington—fitting permanent memorials not only of three Allied leaders but to a great and deserving American portrait painter.

A comment on Cecilia Beaux' ability appears in a letter written to her by the Hon. Joseph Buffington, senior judge of the United States Circuit Court in Philadelphia. Referring to her portrait of a deceased member of the Court, Judge Buffington said, "I don't think I could give you higher evidence of the fact that I really feel his presence in our court deliberations with the same acuteness I used to feel when he sat beside us . . . your brush has portrayed one who, being dead, yet speaketh." * [35]

During her long career Cecilia Beaux was also an instructor in art, and remained on the faculty of the Pennsylvania Academy of the Fine Arts for twenty-one years, from 1895 through 1916. She had the authority to select her own students, and who they may have been is conjecture now. Yet during her time at the Academy such master painters as William Glackens, Charles Demuth, Arthur B. Carles and the great painter John Marin were students at the Academy. Surely she left her impression upon them. [16]

"Fortunate is the pupil," she wrote, "whose master brings with him far more than he personally contains or is aware of, as something communicated. A student's first conception of art should

* Discovery of the above quotation had special interest for one of the authors of this book. Later in his life, Judge Buffington became Frances Neilson's stepfather.

not be delivered to him in small packages. He should find in his masters more than is given to him. Or let him feel only a sense of his relation to art, to the subject, his preceptors only liberating him upon the road, warming his desire toward what he is attempting to do, not showing him the over much and the myriad possibilities of it, but the simplest solution. He must find out the secrets for himself later, if ever." [34]

Cecilia Beaux found a place in New England, at Gloucester, Massachusetts, and built a summer home and studio there. Here for years she spent her summers working, always working, with her color and brushes and palette. It was a beautiful place on the harbor, and held a serenity that reflected well her own personality. Here she could carry on with her secure manner of painting, in peace, regardless of the tumult of change in the world outside her studio. She did not disregard change, or resent it. She recognized it, but it was not a part of her. Cecilia Beaux had the sincerity of always being herself—an achievement for even famous artists.

She died in Gloucester in 1942, at seventy-nine, after a long career, successful enough to be envied by anyone. World War II was underway at the time of her death, and she did not live to know the violent eras to follow.

CECILIA BEAUX'
CONTRIBUTION
TO ART

As a portrait painter, Cecilia Beaux was one of the last of an outstanding succession of Americans including John Singleton Copley, Charles Willson Peale, other Peales, Gilbert Stuart, John Neagle, Thomas Eakins, John Singer Sargent, and James Abbott McNeill Whistler (although Eakins and Whistler were far more general painters than portraitists). For over a century affluent Americans wanted for posterity, and for their own status, portraits of themselves and of their families. With advent of the camera and of new styles in art, portraiture waned in importance. As a fine art, in America at least, it fell into disrepute. Art itself was one thing; painting portraits was another. The expression became current: "One cannot be an artist and a portrait painter at the same time. The two do not go together." There were some who could defy the belief with success, but the general statement was true.

There was a basic reason. Those who did wish portraits to be done wanted them executed in traditions of the past, with dark backgrounds and conventional poses. Meanwhile, the course of other painting moved ahead to experimentation, unconventional forms and ultimately into abstraction. Most painters took to the fields where popularity and the markets lay. Portraiture was left to hacks, and photographers.

This situation was far less true in Europe. European "moderns" did portraits in their own styles, fresh and vibrant. Yet portraits even so were incidental for them. Their work lay mainly in other directions.

Today the state of portrait painting is reversing itself. Portraits in contemporary techniques are becoming accepted, even though in board rooms of corporations and reading rooms of clubs there are still hung paintings of presidents and famous members which are indistinguishable from those of a hundred years ago. One strong influence in modern-day portraiture has been *Time* magazine, which has used more painted portraits and drawings on its weekly covers than it has photographs. The variety of style is deliberate. Likenesses are always there, but the techniques and the results are as different as the many artists commissioned to make them.

As portrait painters, both Mary Cassatt and Cecilia Beaux proved that women could equal if not excel their male counterparts. Whereas Mary Cassatt was concerned with art and its developing forms, Cecilia Beaux contented herself with the individual she was painting: with personality, with the inner character of her sitter, with use of portraiture in its full sense of depiction. She made portraits as art. In these respects, her accomplishments (in the opinion of the authors of this book) exceeded the slick portraits of Sargent. Sargent (in this specific opinion) seems little more than a commercial painter, even though his value appears to be rising at this present moment. Contrarily, his watercolors are superb. Cecilia Beaux never had commercial aspects in mind. She never had to. What she did was of the most sincere quality. Her reward was the commission to do the portraits of World War I heroes, Clemenceau, Mercier, and Beatty.

The portraits of her family and friends perhaps excel in quality those of the three men. She surely had a woman's instinct in interpreting women and children. She may "live" longer for the latter than for the former.

The foregoing comments refer to Cecilia Beaux as a portrait painter, and to portraiture in general. Yet Cecilia was a true

artist, also. Where in this area does she stand? At the beginning
of this section on Cecilia Beaux, it was pointed out that an artist
can be successful without being "advanced." Her whole career, as
she has said herself, marks this basic truth. Perhaps this is Cecilia
Beaux' greatest contribution to the history of art.

One does not have to be "new" to be "good." How many
"new" are not good, and quickly die, in their work?

Cecilia Beaux spent years in her training as her story can tell.
She was thoroughly skilled. She could take one look at the hands
of Cardinal Mercier, and know how to do them. The same thing
happened in the first serious portrait she ever did, of her sister
and the little nephew in "Les derniers jours d'enfance" where
the entwined hands of the mother and child meant so much. It
was only after long years of study and practice that Cecilia would
admit even to herself that she was a professional painter.

She never hit the dramatic heights of her contemporaries. Yet
as an artist, and as a woman, she made a path for others to follow.

One other contribution of Cecilia Beaux to art in general is
her autobiography *Background with Figures*. The book is written beautifully, with perception, depth of understanding, and a
music of words. To read it is a joyful experience.*

ANALYSES OF
REPRODUCED
WORK

As ABOVE explained, the first serious portrait done by Cecilia
Beaux, in her early twenties, of her sister and nephew, aged
three, was the picture to which she gave the dream-like title in
French, "Les derniers jours de l'enfance." How she painted the
portrait has already been briefly described.

After its completion the painting was shown at the Pennsylvania Academy of the Fine Arts, in the room then called the
"North Gallery," now Gallery F. It was on one of the angled corner
panels. Countless paintings have hung there since—modernists,
student's work, and lately Andrew Wyeth's—but so far few have
survived as this one of Cecilia Beaux. Such is the history of the
Pennsylvania Academy, where one has scarcely to walk across
the floor without a record going somewhere into the archives
for all to read in a future time.

This painting, the one to be accepted at the Paris Salon, was
her first true triumph. It is now in the possession of her great-
niece, Mrs. Henry Saltonstall. Cecilia said of it, "It has lasted well,

* *Background with Figures*, Houghton, Mifflin Co., Boston and
New York: 1930.

and its virtues, such as they were, remain; as do its crassy youthfulness, and the naïveté of its composition."

Examining the reproduction of this painting (Plate 15), its virtues, as Cecilia called them, are evident. It may be called a sentimental picture. At this time, and at her age, sentiment was acceptable. She was painting a child still young enough to be content to lie on his mother's lap. In a few more months he would be too restless, and feel foolish. So it was indeed the "Last Days of Infancy." Cecilia caught in her portrait the half-and-half expression of the young boy, content now but not for long. On the other hand, his mother (Cecilia's sister, Aimée) shows the enduring quality of a mother's love.

In composition, there is intuitive understanding. The dark dress of the mother, the wainscoting and table, are offset by the boy's colorful clothing, which pulls the focus of the picture to him. The flowers in the vase pick up the brighter colors, and the direction of the stem turns the gaze inward—a gaze which the section of picture frame in the right hand corner holds from running out on that side and pushes back towards the mother's forehead. From that, the natural lines carry down in circular motion to the child. Again, the sweep of the mother's skirt, and its fold running out across the floor to the right, pulls the eye down and back up to the top of the picture, from where it returns to the focal point—the child.

This sense of composition may have been partly instinctive on Cecilia's part—young as she was—but some of it was surely learned. The highlights, touching briefly the table's side and leg, were other subtle points of good composition.

She may have emphasized too strongly the complex pattern of the rug. She did take advantage of part of the rug design—the angular line in front of the mother's shoes—to help the eye travel up to the vase of flowers. Without that one line in the rug, much of the painting would be lost. But otherwise the pattern on the floor is too much for the rest of the painting to hold. The line across the bottom of the painting, representing the rug's border, is matched by the similar line of the top of the wainscoting. But the carpet on the right, behind the mother's figure on the chair, carries too much detail to offset its opposite, the vase of flowers on the table. If some of that rug design had been simplified, or less complex, like the wainscoting above it, the painting would have been a more rounded "whole."

Yet as it stands, it is her first all-out portrait. Indeed, it has "lasted well."

A portrait done three years later by Cecilia Beaux, then twenty-four, depicted a girl ten years old, Fanny Travis Cochran of Philadelphia (Plate 16). Here is Cecilia in the full height of her technical skill in portraiture. She has caught the innocence of childhood and of the first thoughtfulness of maturity. The drawing is flawless, of the brown hair with bangs, the brown eyes and the mouth. The hand on the chair is perfectly reproduced, and the chair itself is truly real to the point of allowing the absolute feel of real wood. The off-white dress with the yellow sash, is rendered with dexterity and sense of form.

Through the portrait anyone must feel a warm and sympathetic liking for the little girl. She comes out from the picture as *real*.

As mentioned above, this is full evidence of Cecilia Beaux' *technical* skill. However, in this case the painting seems too perfect. As a work of art it appears to miss the subtle quality of living for itself, not just for its subject. The little girl is so carefully posed, so especially dressed for the occasion. The chair is too carefully placed for spontaneity. The draperies of the background are too "set," and too carefully established.

The hand is so carefully and fully drawn that it pulls attention away from the head. So does the chair. This portrait, beautifully done though it is, shows Cecilia Beaux with her least quality as a fine artist. Here she seems to have fallen into the trap of mere portraiture, so easy and commonplace a thing to have happen to painters of portraits.

Once again the difference between portraits as a technique and painting as an art shows itself. The reproduction here illustrates the point. Cecilia Beaux seldom found herself faced with this difference. She was a superb artist as well as portrait painter.

The next portrait is far from these criticisms. This painting, "New England Woman" (Plate 17) was done in 1895, eight years later than the one of the little girl. The subject is Mrs. John Richards of Washington, Connecticut. Here is not only a portrait meant to be such, but a fine painting as well. The lady is sitting in a natural position at her bedroom window facing the light from outdoors. The weather must be warm, because she holds a fan in her hand. Papers are held casually in her lap. Behind her is the bed with pillows.

PLATE 16

Little Girl (Fanny Travis Cochran), by Cecilia Beaux.
The Pennsylvania Academy of the Fine Arts,
Philadelphia.

Cecilia in this painting used her fine sense of composition. The chair, a secondary part of the whole now, gives vertical lines on the right, which are picked up on the left by the vertical window curtains. The verticals frame the upright sitting figure. The horizontal lines of the bed pillow cases are caught up by two rungs of the chair—all the way from the top to the bottom of the painting.

Forms are neatly balanced over the whole composition: the round candlestick and the roundness of the lace cap over the hair of the head, rectangles of books, pillows, and, again, the underpart of the chair. Each part of this painting works together to make a satisfying whole.

The drawing is far more free. The definition of the face is lovely, and never forced. The hands this time are underplayed, so that they become one with the figure, not separate attractions in themselves.

This is the Cecilia Beaux who had the great gift of character interpretation. This portrait foreshadows the many, many portraits she was yet to do.

Just a year earlier than this she painted a self-portrait, a small one of head and shoulders (Plate 14). Considerably later, with her international reputation secure, she was invited to be a candidate for membership in the National Academy of Design in New York. For election, she was requested to present two paintings for acceptance as an Academician. One of the two was the self-portrait here reproduced.

In this portrait she did an interpretation of what she believed in. She painted her head high, her gaze straight and clear. Her shoulders are swung back. Her pose is calm, confident; her mouth compassionate. She knew what she wanted to be. She knew herself.

She was handsome, beautiful in her own simplicity. She did not underestimate herself. Why should she? Any artist or writer who plays down his own confidence in himself betrays his own work and effort.

The most effective touch in this self-portrait is the level line of her upper eyelids. In just this one seemingly insignificant detail she told the world exactly what she felt, what she wanted, and what she intended. Without that level line of the upper lids, she would have been quite a different person. Hold a pencil point over her left eyelid and notice the difference.

She was not looking at herself when she painted the por-

PLATE 17

A New England Woman, by Cecilia Beaux.
The Pennsylvania Academy of the Fine Arts,
Philadelphia.

trait. Most artists use a mirror, and their reproductions of themselves are front view, face-to-face so to speak. This portrait is at a three-quarter angle. How did she do that? Only by knowing herself—without need of a mirror. She more than surmounted the difficulty of a self-portrait.

Obviously she was elected to membership in the National Academy, and could thereafter attach the initials "N.A." to her name. The painting is in the Academy's collection in New York.

This happened to be the third self-portrait which Cecilia Beaux painted. One she did as a girl, the second when she was in her late twenties. This third portrait, reproduced, was painted when she was thirty-one.

In 1925, years later, she was asked by the Italian Royal Minister of Public Instruction to paint a self-portrait for the Medici Collection in the Uffizi Gallery in Florence. She was the first American woman to receive this invitation. She did the painting, her fourth of herself.

Of the seven great women painters in this book, Cecilia Beaux is one of three to be represented in the great gallery by self-portraits. The other two women are Angelica Kauffmann and Elisabeth Vigée-Lebrun.

Cecilia Beaux' ability and understanding of her art never ceased to grow. In 1902 she did an informal portrait of her brother-in-law, Dr. Henry Sturgis Drinker (Color Plate 5). The title of the painting is very simply, "Man with the Cat." Even the title reveals its simplicity. In this portrait there are no pretensions, no false moves, no weakness of drawing or color or composition. It shows Cecilia at the peak of an artist's competence.

A man in a white suit sits on a dark chair, against a light background. The lines of the background supplement the figure, and even though the window panels are carefully drawn, they stay in the background. The chair, the suit, collar and tie are all secondary to the essential purpose. Three areas of the painting stand out, in reverse order: one sees the man's hands, strong, long-fingered and gaunt; one's eye goes to the head of the cat, so realistic with sleepy eyes and relaxed ears and paws; but then one looks to the head, face and eyes of the man. Here behind the bushy mustache and sideburns, the strong emphatic character of the subject himself takes over the painting.

Cecilia Beaux used a light from her left to bring out most of the forms of the head and figure. A slight secondary lighting from the right establishes more definitely the outline of the head. The forehead and eyes are drawn with exactness. The result is that the man himself becomes extraordinarily vital. The artist has, through her skill, let herself take second place. The portrait stands free of its own creator.

Earlier it was stated that Cecilia Beaux may have achieved her best results in portraits of her family. This "Man with the Cat" is an example. Any painter should do better when relaxed and does not try too hard. Yet, does this general statement really mean that much? It does, when the artist is thoroughly aware of the skill required, and technique at last becomes a matter of "second nature." We can be sure that Cecilia Beaux enjoyed painting "Man with the Cat," and that she did not worry about her own ability to create her subject's character on canvas.

The painting of Admiral Sir David Beatty, Lord Beatty, is different. This portrait has been referred to earlier; it was one of the three World War I portraits commissioned as a climax to Cecilia Beaux' career. Along with those of Cardinal Mercier and Premier Clemenceau this work is in the National Collection of Fine Arts of The Smithsonian Institution, Washington.

As a portrait it is strong, dynamic, a powerful representation of the British Naval Commander who was responsible for smashing the great German Fleet at the Battle of Jutland. Cecilia Beaux painted him in full dress uniform with sword. She added the background of stormy sea and a wild sky, with the smoke and fire of a raging naval fight across the horizon.

It is a spectacular presentation of a spectacular and remarkable man. Is portrait painting *really* fine art? This rendition is as great a proof as any painter as qualified as Cecilia Beaux could produce. No camera could truly catch the Admiral's personality, no ordinary draftsman could bring out the personality of one of England's great heroes of all time as Cecilia Beaux has done in paint.

The portrait of Admiral Lord Beatty is a posed, formal delineation of a man. The "Man with the Cat" is informal, natural. The two together show the wide range of Cecilia Beaux' understanding of translating human nature into art.

A final question: How could a woman know enough about a man to paint with brush and color the strength of Admiral Lord Beatty as she did in this painting? The answer seems to be: could anyone *except* a woman understand a man so well?

123

PLATE 18

Admiral Sir David Beatty, Lord Beatty 1871–1936,
by Cecilia Beaux. *National Collection of Fine Arts,
Smithsonian Institution, Washington, D.C.,
gift of the National Art Committee.*

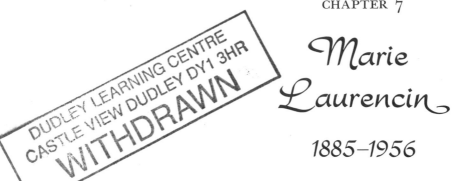

Marie Laurencin

1885–1956

HEN a girl graduates from school at the age of twenty and decides to take up porcelain painting, what does one expect? Especially after her art instructor at school tells her that she would be wiser to learn the mandolin?

This story proves that nothing or no one is beyond the hope of dreaming. For so began the career of Marie Laurencin, the painter who became known world-wide for her individualistic art that evolved from her own fantasy world. Long-limbed girls, deer, and birds were creatures of her fanciful world, hazy and unreal in her pictorial expressions of them, but so alike to everyone's dreams that they became so real, as never, once seen, to be forgotten.

To trace the personal details of Marie Laurencin's life is difficult. She is almost too contemporary. The fragments can be gathered, but she lives on in the work that she left. It is so unlike any other that a glance alone reveals, "There is Marie Laurencin."

She began slowly. Marie was born in Paris in 1885. That city was her lifetime home. She went to school conventionally, and graduated from the Lycée Lamartine in 1905. Her art studies at school, however, were too unconventional to satisfy her teacher who was led to give the advice about learning to play the mandolin.[38]

Chastened but undaunted, she entered an art school called the Académie Humbert.

YOUNG GIRL
OF
MONTMARTRE

125

Normally, this could have been the end of Marie Laurencin. Perhaps she would have been lost in commercial art, or ended as a hobbyist, painting porcelain dishes for her home.

Destiny determined differently. At the same school was a student named Georges Braque, five years older than Marie, a young man just beginning to make his way as an artist. He was growing beyond art schools. He saw Marie's work and said, in effect, "This is no place for either of us. Let's get out." [39]

BATEAU-LAVOIR

IF EVER there was a period of time in art history that could be called adventurous, stirring, and romantic, it was the decade that began around 1904 in Paris. A tourist can still visit a tiny square in the Montmartre quarter, in the shadow of the great white church of the Sacre Coeur on the hill overlooking the whole of the city. The square, where one can drink an apéritif and dwell in historic memories, is at the foot of a narrow street called rue Ravignan. At the upper end of the little street is a strange building or combination of buildings. The place was known as the *Bateau-Lavoir,* so nicknamed from the boats on the Seine where Parisienne women used to do their washing. The resemblance came from constant leaks all through the building, or buildings, with every rain.

The *Bateau-Lavoir* had been inhabited by poor working-men, old seamstresses, and persons unable to afford better living quarters. One, two, or three artists found accommodations and settled into studio space there at a cost which suited their meager pocketbooks. One of these was a young, fiery Spaniard, Pablo Picasso.

At this time, 1904, the art world of Paris was once again being swept by a great wave of restlessness. The Impressionist Revolution of 1875–1886 (approximate dates) had died out and been succeeded by the Neo-Impressionists led by Georges Seurat. This group tried—and succeeded—in capitalizing on the free, informal painting of light initiated by Edouard Manet (see section on Berthe Morisot in this book), and carried on by Claude Monet and the distinguished Impressionist painters. With the final dissolution of this movement into separate ways, many painters became individualists in their own right, like Cézanne and Degas. Younger ones, however, wanted to build on the spontaneous brushwork created by the Impressionists and turn the idea of "light" into more formal and classic uses. The style

126

known as "pointillism" was created by Seurat, Signac, and others. Some of the older Impressionists joined in, like Camille Pissaro, an outstanding painter who never quite made the grade in his own time but was always searching. The Neo-Impressionists influenced many upcoming artists including Matisse.*

Yet by 1904 and 1905 even the Neo-Impressionist momentum faded. Cézanne had retreated to southern France. Gauguin had died on a South Pacific island. A new set of young painters poured into Paris from all over Europe, England and the United States. They were restless, searching, ready to build again. On what? Toward what? They did not know, but they experimented to find answers for the tremendous future which they instinctively felt lay ahead.

One result was a violent use of color, breaking down lines and realistic expression into relations of form for its own sake. Abstract art was being born.

A segment of the new painters based their work on Gauguin's findings of color designs, and went far ahead of what he ever dreamed. A group of them together were labeled "Les Fauves," the Wild Beasts. Matisse was one, and so were Derain, Othon Friesz, and Braque. The Wild Beasts did not endure long as a movement in art. Those involved were too independent, and carried on further individualism.

One who did not become identified with the Fauves was the Spaniard, Picasso. At the time he moved into the *Bateau-Lavoir* buildings in 1904, he was nearing the end of his "Blue Period," of figure paintings. Predominately young painters gathered around him, and slowly Picasso began to emerge as a leader. The *Bateau-Lavoir,* its little street and neighboring cafes became a focal point and meeting place for the struggling ones, the new painters who sought new ways. Older, established painters remained in the studios near the boulevards. On the hill of Montmartre, under the shadows of the great white church, the future was being hatched.

In the shop of an art dealer named Clovis Sagot, one of the first dealers to buy anything by Picasso, Marie Laurencin met Picasso and his friend Apollinaire, the Italian-born writer and poet who expressed the literary side of the new art movements.[8]

* Refer: Guggenheim Museum Exhibition of Neo-Impressionism in the spring of 1968, organized by Professor Robert L. Herbert of Yale University, with catalogue written by him.

Georges Braque had met Picasso, too—he had taken a studio in the Montmartre area—and with Braque, Marie joined the circle. From that moment she was an artist, also.

She was a girl with long, narrow face, slanting eyelids, a full mouth and curly hair. (See Self-Portrait, drawing, Plate 19.) Parenthetically, it is remarkable how many of her subsequent paintings of girls had her own characteristics.

Marie Laurencin had fallen into the most fascinating band of young artists who, probably, have ever gathered themselves together. They worked in their studios during the day, and in the evening met over coffee in the little cafés. All of them were there—most of the names that ring today as the great innovators of the twentieth century: Picasso, Braque, Fantin-Latour, Derain, the writer Apollinaire. Who else? Friesz, Raoul Dufy, Vlaminck, Van Dongen, those who made these years the great ones of French art.[8] Matisse lived in another section of Paris, and moved in a different direction. He, too, emerged as a leader of another group, equally bold. He opened a studio-school in central Paris, and developed in his work from the Fauves influence toward his own decorative compositions.

The American writer Gertrude Stein was one who supported both groups. She was already in Paris, writing her own strange sentences, with their measured rhythms that in themselves had a startling effect on American styles of writing. "A rose is a rose is a rose." What Gertrude Stein's final influence may be no one knows now. Today she has faded, unjustly. "Four Saints in Three Acts," the opera with libretto by Gertrude Stein and with music by Deems Taylor, is a classic that has been revived and should be more often.

Gertrude Stein was one of the first to buy a painting from Marie Laurencin.[38] She supported both Matisse and Picasso, and was the one to introduce them to each other for the first time. Matisse showed Picasso samples of African primitive art, which led the latter into his new period of Negro experimentation.[8]

During the evenings at the cafés Marie listened to the discussions and arguments about art. Little did she, or any one of them realize that they were creating a revolutionary movement in French art up there on the side of the Paris hill.

The movement was such that no artist today, however far out, can truthfully say that he does not owe something to Picasso's group who met each evening under the stars to argue

PLATE 19

Self-portrait, by Marie Laurencin.
Collection, The Museum of Modern Art, New York.

about the future art. The principal painters did the talking. Others came to listen around the edges. No wonder that Paris, and its section of Montmartre became glamorous to students all over the world.

During those evenings Pablo Picasso and Georges Braque talked of Cubism, a new way of interpreting art. Some listened and understood. Others never comprehended at all. Picasso's ideas developed little by little. Maybe his explanations at cafés and over coffee in the evenings helped him, too. Soon he was involved in Cubism as a style of painting, breaking his subjects into geometrical patterns. With him was Braque. The two were the real innovators of Cubistic compositions.[8]

They drew, however, upon Paul Cézanne, who was the first one to see that forms could be broken into cubes, cones, and other geometric shapes. In his perceptions, he was one of the three founders of modern art as we know it today. (The other two: Mondrian, the Dutchman, who did lines and squares in geometric patterns of color; and Kandinsky, the German, who splashed out color compositions in glowing designs and set the pace for the later New York Abstract Expressionists.)

Meanwhile, Cézanne died in 1906. The newspapers castigated him in their obituaries, one critic complaining that nothing he had ever done could be considered a work of art.[8]

Picasso, however, along with Braque, picked up Cézanne's ideas and carried them forward. The Spanish artist has been for the many years of his life the outstanding draftsman of the human figure in the classic sense. He knows better how to draw than almost any other artist ever has. Can one see *that* in his paintings of the last few years? Actually, yes. Even the most non-objective pictures still indicate form, and form comes from knowledge of drawing.

It is told of Picasso, and it could have been about this time, that he was ready to change his style of painting. His studio was full of things unsold. There was no room left to move around, and he needed space to start new paintings. So he called in a dealer, and struck a bargain. Picasso sold everything he had for a price reputedly of less than twenty dollars for each painting. Many of the paintings were of the so-called "Blue Period" and included those which have since become nearly priceless. Yet to Picasso at that time the arrangement was a good one. He managed to get his paintings out on the market instead of keeping

them in his studio. He had funds with which to buy materials
and supplies to start a new style of painting. His studio was
cleared, and he had space. Incidently, it is also told that it
took the art dealer two whole days to move out all the work
from the studio, using boys pushing handcarts through the
streets of Paris.

Again and again one sees or hears of painters who maintain
stubborn pride in an artificial price standard of their work. A
work of art is worth exactly what someone is willing to pay
for it and no more. That price level, conforming to the basic
laws of economics, is frequently ignored by artists, especially
beginning ones. They believe that the higher the price they
set on themselves, the more important they will be considered.
Sometimes it is true, under unusual circumstances, but usually
it is not. When Picasso cleared out his studio at minimum sale
prices, he did not set his reputation back very far.

No one of those artists and writers who met nightly to hear
themselves and others talk foresaw what those magic moments of
the *Bateau-Lavoir* would bring to the world. They worked, and
created paintings in new and different ways, all sparked by intensity of enthusiasm. Cubism burst into full expression, shattering forever the necessity for literal rendition of any subject
or idea. Color, composition, the painting for its own sake were
the watchwords. Art was leaping forward.

Marie Laurencin was caught up by the enthusiasm, too. She
did not respond to Cubism. She did paintings of people in a
style that was still tentative and tight. Some of her paintings
recorded the artists of the *Bateau-Lavoir*. One included a group
of four: Picasso, Fernande Oliver, a friend of Picasso, who was
writing about him even then, the writer Apollinaire, and Marie
herself.

Along with the others, she showed her paintings in the Salon
des Independents. This was the annual unjuried exhibition open
to all that had grown up over the years in opposition to the
traditional Paris Salon of the academicians. The Independents
show was an outgrowth of the early Impressionist annual exhibitions, born under trying circumstances. Marie Laurencin's first
appearance was in 1906, a year when the show contained five
thousand, five hundred entries. (Some references insist her first
year was 1907, a minor discrepancy as the 1907 show was equally
brilliant, and still had five thousand, four hundred entries.) [8]

131

Through these glorious years the arts burst into bloom on every hand. Isadora Duncan danced in Paris. Debussy and Ravel were introducing new innovations in music. Diaghilev brought his Russian Ballet to the French capital. In writing, literature was creating a stir equal to that of the fine arts. Modigliani had come to Paris. The circle on the Montmartre hill discovered Rousseau, the older man who painted almost without any art training at all. His were principally jungle pictures—primitive after a fashion—which he claimed he remembered from his youthful soldier's experience in Mexico. His painting of a nude girl sleeping on a couch under palms and jungle growth with wild animals lying peacefully around her created a sensation. (Rousseau's stories of Mexico are open to some question, if indeed he ever went there at all.) Rousseau, called *Le Douanier,* the customs man, because that had been his lifetime career before turning to painting, astounded everyone. The group of the *Bateau-Lavoir* welcomed him to their midst. He explained the girl on the couch merely by calling the painting "A Dream."

Apollinaire, the poet, wrote verses to everyone—to Rousseau, on the occasion of a banquet in his honor which went on in spite of the fact that Picasso ordered the food for the wrong day; to Marie whose good friend now was the poet. Gertrude Stein wrote about all of them including herself: "Everybody called Gertrude Stein, Gertrude . . . everybody called Picasso, Pablo and Fernande, Fernande and everybody called Guillaume Apollinaire, Guillaume and Max Jacob, Max but everybody called Marie Laurencin, Marie Laurencin." They all went to the circus, which Picasso loved, and often afterward drifted on to the cafés of Montparnasse.

So much of the glamor of Paris to artists and art students centered around that circle on the hill of Montmartre that the memory must always linger. Stories of painters—starving in cold garrets while the snow drifted over rooftops—and masterpieces created beside the charcoal stoves were true then. Tales of models and the men who painted them, of the *grisettes* who shared the lives and made breakfasts for the dedicated ones were true, too. It was a beautiful and wonderful time, and none of it was false because the works of art from that period have become renowned. Not all, because from among any group of artists some will live longer and others will be soon forgotten. The *Bateau-Lavoir* average was far higher in ultimate success than probably any group at any time.

IT ENDED suddenly, when in 1914 the German armies rolled across Belgium and the French borders. Perhaps that group of artists on the hill would have stopped painting anyway, or wound up in disagreements. No matter—the war answered any doubts.

The painters moved out. Picasso, earning money, had already gone. Only hangers-on remained, and the cafés ever since have merely echoed the sharp arguments of those who discussed fiercely where art would turn, what was truth out of the past, how to search out the essential existence of art itself.

Many of the French painters were caught up in the war. Paris was left to the foreigners. Marie Laurencin herself married a German shortly before World War I. With its outbreak, she found herself under French law classified as carrying her husband's nationality. Marie, thoroughly Parisienne, was suddenly an alien in her own home. She was forced to leave for Spain, where she stayed through the war.

After the war much of the past was gone, but still another generation joined with the remaining older one to carry on newer experimentation. The Dadaists, who tried to sweep away everything, existed for a time. The Surrealists came into being, following an earlier lead by de Chirico, an Italian, and Chagall, a Russian. Yet the painters already established moved into their own orbits, less dependent on others. Picasso carried on with one great leap after another, as if from rock to rock. Braque was more committed to following Cubism than Picasso ever was. Raoul Dufy took up the cheerful scenes of street and seashore and made bright parodies of them.

Marie Laurencin, back from Spain and with a terminated marriage, went her way, too. She ignored Cubism, and all the other "isms" that were sprouting right and left, and found her own world for expression in her paintings.

A popular fad swept over Paris. The current craze for a time was to sing and hear songs of folklore and fable, sung in every café and on each street corner. What the songs were and how their words read mattered little. They were soon forgotten. Marie Laurencin listened, and in her they awakened some kind of response before then untouched.

Folklore—fable—imagination—dreams—fantasy—Marie's alert mind jumped from one to another. She began to paint all over again, fresh and new. A whole world of her own sprang into life, and pictures flowed from her brushes. Each piece of work was so individually Marie Laurencin that no one could ever make the mistake of not knowing who did it.

She painted girls, girls with guitars or mandolins, girls singly and in groups, compositions of girls' figures, portraits of girls, girls with horses. Sometimes there were deer in her paintings, beautiful, slim does like the girls, sometimes there were birds.

She is reported as having asked once, "Why should I paint dead fish, onions and beer glasses? Girls are so much prettier." [42]

Marie was French. An American would never have said that.

The daughter of the *concierge* was the model for many of her paintings. Her girls, even done from models, had a peculiar unreality. They floated in air, really flat in drawing of form, and yet they were very real. Marie found the key to her work when she discovered eyes. Her girls' eyes were alike but not alike—meaning that in technique of handling they were characteristic of Laurencin, but individually they had their own distinctions. The eyes were Laurencin's. They made her paintings what they are.

The critic Andre Salmon reported of Marie Laurencin, that she could paint "young girls with eyes like does, and does with the apprehensions of virgins." [39] Yet the eyes were sensuous, haunting, and impossible to forget. She made them dark, with eyelids slanting over their roundness. Lips were full, but faces were long and narrow as her own. Limbs of her girls flattened out, like the wispy fantasies she created. In color, she turned to grays, pinks, pale greens, and blues. People said she used pastel colors. This was actually not true, as pastels can be dark and brilliant, as wide in range as any medium. She used oils on canvas, watercolor, and etchings, more than she ever worked with pastel crayons. The subtle colors of her palette only reflected the elusive figures of her subjects. The style of painting was muted, hazy almost, giving to Marie Laurencin's work the feeling that maybe the picture itself wasn't there.

Yet her paintings were very much there, on the walls of galleries and homes of collectors in Europe and increasingly in America. Her popularity grew after World War I, and it did not diminish. One can almost say that she "floated" through the tumultuous period of French art of the 1920's—floated because she was with it but not actually a part of it. In her winsome way she was purely Marie Laurencin.

She showed her paintings in Paris regularly, and included a representative collection in a historic exposition of Masters of Independent Art held in 1937 at the Petit Palais. There were exhibitions in New York and elsewhere. In 1928 she won an honorable mention at the Carnegie International in Pittsburgh, then one of the most important annual shows of world-wide art.

The steady outpouring of Marie's black-eyed girls in oils on canvas, watercolors on paper, in etchings and lithographs were not all that she did. Under a commission from Diaghilev she did sets and costumes for productions of the Ballet Russe, where her girls and deer and birds could play in glorious abandon over whole backdrops in the theater. She did settings for the stage of the Comédie Française as well. Finally, one of her major achievements was as an illustrator for books, among them *Alice in Wonderland*. The magic of Lewis Carroll in combination with the fanciful dream-world of Marie Laurencin blended beautifully.

Her popularity and reputation continued until June, 1956, when, at the age of 70, she came to the end of her long, exciting, fruitful, and artistically romantic career. She had lived through the great days of French art. Her own work carried on unflaggingly even when, in the 1930's, French art as a whole began to disintegrate in the unhappy period before World War II.

Years before her death, Frank Crowninshield, one of the most discerning and able collectors and critics of art in New York City, wrote in the catalogue of a show given her at the Findlay Galleries the ultimate in perceptive interpretation. He said that Marie Laurencin, a favorite of his, was "following instinctively the impulses of an undivided feminine psyche." He described what he called "that underworld of her spirit so miraculously peopled by white peonies, doves, and pale ladies, all living together mystically, or in a garden of dreams. And those ladies of hers—for they are unmistakably ladies—how enchanting they are, with their undefined pools of night which are their eyes, their magnolia-soft cheeks, their plumes of periwinkle blue and lips of fadeless rose." [40] A fine salute to a great and individual artist!

To ATTEMPT a definitive forecast of Marie Laurencin's place in the future judgment of art history is more difficult than with other women in this book. Bluntly, she has not been dead long enough. Popular though she was during her lifetime, is there currently a re-assessment of her work as a painter?

Some authorities think this may be true, at the moment at least. There is no question that for the three or four decades after World War I—in the twenties, thirties, forties, and fifties, she was an immensely popular painter. Her pictures were everywhere, always distinguished by her own special style. Since her death in 1956, there has naturally been a tapering off in gallery exhibitions. There is no longer a new supply coming into the market.

This phase of an artist's career can be most critical. He—or she—has completed his total life's work. There is no more to come for further evaluation. The record must stand on its own.

The result can vary from one extreme to another, depending upon the individual. The production of a highly renowned artist may, after his death, become more in demand and consequently higher priced because nothing more will be coming from him. Even so, this extra popularity can be short-lived, and fade under competition from a new generation. In other cases his contemporary reputation may be revalued after an artist dies, and second thoughts may push him into a limbo—once again falling to live competition. Yet often an artist, who has for a time been out of favor, will return strongly in popular esteem.

Dead or alive, artists are subject to the same kind of intangible factors that affect the stock markets. External factors, combinations of events, later trends in styles—these plus the unguessable shifting of public opinion can make or break an artist's reputation and demand for his works. It may be unfair, but it is true.

However, unlike the stock markets where a certain corporate stock, once dead, usually remains dead, an artist no longer popular after death has a host of historians, dealers and collectors anxious to bring him back again if he has any possibilities at all for study or for commercial profit. Frequently in recent times an artist considered forgotten for fifty or more years has suddenly been "discovered" and brought back.

Marie Laurencin does not fit into any of the classifications described above. A gallery on 57th Street in New York has just reported that there is a steady demand for her paintings as they become available for prices up to $30,000 each, depending on quality and size of the work. Yet some of the public has forgotten, or never knew her name.

She was an artist who followed no group or clique, and who established no following or school of her own. She was entirely individual. She has been, in a sense, timeless for she could have painted as well in another era. A critic some years ago expressed this idea: "Infatuated as we are with the importance of our epoch we take it too much for granted that a Marie Laurencin belongs to our time. Yet she may appear as baffling to the generations after us. To them she will probably seem a wisp of ether in the era of volumes and geometry. When she exhibited for the first time in 1907 (note: actually 1906) at the Salon des Independents many felt the shock of this contrast. 'She is in bad company,' said the adversaries of modern art. But rebellious youth claimed as its own a talent fresh, original and unadulterated by any contact. . . . All that Marie Laurencin paints is like a fairy tale. . . . Who are these goddesses and nymphs? Everything is a secret with Marie Laurencin. . . . And all this is enfolded in an atmosphere as luminous and unreal as Marie Laurencin alone can paint. Few artists have ever been so delicate and bold at the same time, or created an art at once so ephemeral and important." [41]

Emily Genauer, noted New York critic, found the same independence on Marie Laurencin's part. Writing on her during her lifetime, Miss Genauer said of the artist's contacts with the early School of Paris group, "Marie did not stay long within their aura. Fearful, perhaps, that the titans would submerge her entirely, convinced that her own personality was essentially feminine and exquisite rather than intellectual and dynamic, she swept clear of their sphere of influence, and developed what she considered as her true character as an artist. The results are extremely well known. Everywhere today one sees her blue and gray rose confections, flat decorations of fluttering, wraith-like women whose ancestors are the ladies in Persian miniatures, 18th century prints, and even the profile pastels of Manet." [40]

It is an attribute and not a fault that Marie Laurencin went her own way, not following the tenets of her friends whom she knew so well. This was sincerity. She found her own world to interpret, that world of dark-eyed girls with long slim arms, of hazy landscapes in geometric forms which could have gone back to Cézanne but were totally unlike the Cézanne precepts followed by Picasso and Braque at the same time.

What other painters have gone their own individual way without following the developing trends, and have created their own

137

individualism? One thinks first of the American, Andrew Wyeth. Laurencin and Wyeth have nothing in common except the asset of individuality. In this respect they are comparable. Wyeth has attained popularity, almost unprecedented in the history of art. Will this reputation hold as time goes by? Undoubtedly he will maintain a position of importance and he deserves to do so, although there may be some adjustment in critical thinking.

Marie Laurencin never reached the peaks Wyeth or her contemporaries Picasso, Braque, and some of the others associated with her, did. Nevertheless, she did achieve popularity and a definite reputation.

In this writing, the opinion is ventured that Marie Laurencin was not only a great woman painter but also an artist who will always be given an excellent rating by future scholars and historians for her place in the School of Paris era. Considered carefully in the light of her work and record, the sense of this book is that she is one of the "greats" of all time, and will always be so placed.

It will not matter whether she was part of the development of "modern" art, which she was not. She could actually be as renowned if she were starting her career today, or tomorrow. She did need the background of the Impressionists, the Neo-Impressionists, the Fauves and the whole liberal attitude of the early twentieth century to grow in, as did Picasso and Matisse and so many others. That she took a highly individualistic path means only that she could have been as well recognized in today's art, or in tomorrow's, as she was accepted in her own recent past.

Marie Laurencin dreamed, and her dreams turned to the reality of her work. When critics found traces of primitive art, of the Persian miniatures, of oriental and Russian influences, they were right. But somehow one feels that Marie would have painted in the same way if she had never known any of these historic backgrounds.

She learned from Cézanne. Some of the Cubist and Surrealist discussions in the coffee bars of Montmartre and Montparnasse rubbed off on her. Otherwise, she was her own in her individualistic creations. The long-armed, long-legged girls with the dark eyes, the birds, dogs, and geometric landscapes belonged only to Marie Laurencin.

Beside her work itself, she will always be remembered for her association with the remarkable era in which she lived. Imagine the career of any young girl and woman close to Picasso, Braque, Dufy, Gertrude Stein, Derain, and later Diaghilev, Stravinsky, the great and near-great in Paris through the years that made the French capital the center of art, music, dance, literature during nearly a half century until Paris itself had to yield precedence to New York and to London. What more wonderful era could be for a girl to live through, despite wars, depressions, and external troubles!

Marie Laurencin was a painter utterly French, and absolutely feminine in the character of her work. She, as much as any others, proved the essential female quality in the great art produced by women.

REPRODUCED in this book is a self-portrait of Marie Laurencin, done in 1906 when she was twenty-one years old and in the same year when she first exhibited in the Salon des Independents (Plate 19). It is a pencil drawing—charcoal pencil, clearly.

This is a noteworthy drawing of herself, executed at the beginning of Marie's association with the group of "Les Fauves." It was a time of new rebellion of young painters, a period of searching for new truths. The drawing reflects the influence of the specific and frank styles then contemporary.

It is not a drawing which shows her to be a pretty girl. All pretensions are stripped away. It is factual, in showing Marie as she truly was—in her own opinion, at least. We must feel that her self-judgment was right. She had dark hair, dark eyes, a thin slanting face narrowing down to the chin. The angle of the lower jaw at the cheek is clearly defined. The two eyes do not exactly match; Marie had surely learned in art school that the eyes of a person are generally dissimilar. The underlip on the left is somewhat overdrawn, an error which pulls the lip slightly away from the face. Otherwise, the drawing is well-balanced and simple.

This drawing of herself is remarkable for one special feature. As mentioned earlier, all the slender dark-eyed girls of her later paintings, for which she became famous, have the same narrow oval head structure. It is almost as if she saw herself in all the models from whom she subsequently drew.

The portrait indicates her early ability in drawing and handling form with charcoal.

The lithograph, "1898—The First Renault Car" (Plate 20), reveals Marie's light touch and sense of humor. Not much of the early automobile appears, and what does cannot have been very realistic. But the group of entranced people have innocent charm, an attribute of Marie's personality.

Notice in this lithograph the sure and adept use of the simplest lines. Each figure is brought to life with a minimum line. The whippet dog is a masterpiece of delineation. So is the nearer girl, and the expressions on the faces of the others. Marie Laurencin used shading only as a supplement to the lines. Much of the shading is done with cross-hatching, a kind of shading which requires great skill. Cross-hatching is apt to result in a disturbing design of X's with the danger of distracting the eye from the drawing itself. In this case Marie Laurencin avoided the danger, and in fact deliberately used a cross-hatched design for the car radiator. This shading does pull attention to the car, and acts as a focal point in the composition of the whole group.

The reproduction in black and white is made from the original lithograph in color. Color lithography is a form of graphic art that requires a special experience and ability to carry out successfully. Besides her painting, Marie Laurencin was well-known for her illustrations for books. The rendition of the Renault is a prime example of her light-hearted approach.

The date of "1898" on the title of the lithograph can be misleading. She must have done it years later, for in that year Marie Laurencin was thirteen. It is not likely that a child of that age would have created a color lithograph of this caliber, and we do remember the remark of her teacher at school that she ought to forget art and take up music. The year 1898 presumably referred back to the date of the Renault's first appearance, perhaps in a magazine—an assumption justified by the vagueness and inaccuracy of the drawing of the car.

When she moved into her own created world of black-eyed maidens, deer, birds and fantasies that never were, Marie Laurencin's paintings in oils and pastels poured out as the flood from a mountain stream. The simile is appropriate and intentional. As backgrounds to her fabulous creatures Marie often used backgrounds of nature: trees, hills, mountains. Such a one is "Nymph and Hind," a painting when the landscape nearly—but not quite —takes over from her figures (Plate 21).

The word *hind* means a doe, the female deer, as compared to the male *stag* of the European red deer. Many painters other than Marie Laurencin have consistently used deer as subjects, but she

PLATE 20

The First Renault Car, by Marie Laurencin.
Collection, The Museum of Modern Art, New York.

PLATE 21

Nymph and Hind, 1925, by Marie Laurencin.
Collection of Philadelphia Museum of Art.

did so in a way especially her own. This painting reproduced is rather more heavy, perhaps more pretentious, than others. In feeling she was lighter, more subtle and rewarding when her figures were close-ups rather than parts of a landscape composition. "Nymph and Hind" is typical Marie Laurencin, but more in parts than in whole.

"Les Deux Amies," the two friends (Color Plate 6), is far more representative of the work which brought fame to her as one of the great women painters. Her two girls, typical Laurencin ones, sit under the branches of a tree. It seems to be a casual painting, but a study of its composition proves that it is not.

The leftward slant of the two figures is countered by the leaning tree trunk behind and above them. Yet the downward push of the foliage helps the upward insistence of the girls' bodies toward their heads. The forms on the far left of the painting seem to hold the two up-and-down oblique drives. The whole composition is simple enough, but subtle in its execution. Studied closely, there are a succession of directions and counter-directions, each interwoven with the others.

Marie Laurencin's colors in her paintings have often been referred to as "pastel." This is really a misstatement of fact, although she did tend toward soft pinks, greens and blues. The term "pastel colors" is a misnomer, as pastel crayons used for painting can be as dark or brilliant as any other materials. When Marie Laurencin actually used pastels, which she often did, she caught the brilliance of flowers and of costume, and the darks of eyes and backgrounds as easily as if she were using oil.

Both the "Nymph and Hind" and "Les Deux Amies" are painted in oil. The earlier one, dated 1925, is typical of her work in mid-career. The second, painted in 1950 when she was sixty-five years old, is an excellent example of the girls whom she painted so profusely.

Always unique, always personal, creating from her own sense of fun and good humor, Marie Laurencin left for the world's enjoyment a special note of cheerfulness to the story of art. All through her life she remained the girl of Paris, one who loved what she did and was loved for it.

PLATE 22

Georgia O'Keeffe.
Pencil sketch by Winthrop Neilson.

CHAPTER 8

Georgia O'Keeffe

1887–

"Direct as an
Arrow and
Hugely Independent"

WHEN Georgia O'Keeffe was a little girl, her mother read stories to her about the Wild West. She listened avidly, and remembered them more than any other stories.[49]

Now, even the mention of Georgia O'Keeffe's name evokes an imagery of the West: whitened bones of steers on desert land, the red walls of canyons, the subtleties of color in cactus flowers. But no cowboys, no Indians, no buffalo hunts—no people. Her paintings do not show human beings. She seeks for her painting the elementary core of nature—the "things other people do not see."

Georgia O'Keeffe's name recalls, however, far more than the West which she has always loved. She has been an abstract artist, and a realist. She was a forerunner of the so-called "hard edge school," popular in contemporary painting. Above all, she is an individualist of her own making who has fulfilled the true measure of personal expression, so seldom achieved by any *artist*— and this word "artist" is here used in its broadest sense. In other words, Georgia O'Keeffe has touched the rare atmosphere of a misused word—genius. She is good.

Not the least of her influence on American art has been the remarkable part she played on the New York scene during the 1920's and 1930's as the wife of Alfred Stieglitz. Stieglitz was the man who introduced modern French art to America even before the famous Armory Show in 1913. He was the man who made a fine art of photography. Stieglitz, with his own gallery, pro-

145

foundly changed the course of American art. He helped the careers of a number of leading artists, but most of all, through a special radiance of personality, he affected the lives of innumerable persons.[45]

Georgia O'Keeffe was born in Wisconsin, at a place called Sun Prairie, in 1887. Her family later moved to Virginia, but meanwhile **Georgia** displayed an amazing precocity. Before she was seventeen, she had studied at Chicago's Art Institute, at New York's Art Students' League, and had held a self-supporting job in Chicago as a commercial artist. Her teacher at the League was William Chase, strictly academic, and as a result of his teaching she won a prize.[49]

Dissatisfied with commercial art and with the strictures of academic instruction, she came to study art at Columbia University in 1914—the year she was seventeen. Here she met another girl who became a long-time friend and, by circumstance, a key to Georgia's whole future. Her name was Anita Pollitzer, and she and Georgia, along with another student, were considered by their instructor better than the rest of the class and set off by themselves. While the other students drew antique casts, the three were permitted to work on their own still-life paintings. At that time, Anita recorded, Georgia lived in a four-dollar-a-week hall bedroom, with only a pot of red geraniums on the fire escape for decoration. She had little money, and spent most of it on art supplies. Yet even then, wrote Anita Pollitzer, Georgia was different. She used brighter colors, a cleaner palette, and better brushes than her classmates. "There was something insatiable about her," her friend said, "as direct as an arrow and hugely independent." [49]

Perhaps no description of Georgia O'Keeffe could be more accurate. Yet the description can probably be broadened by saying that Miss O'Keeffe is intensely preoccupied by nature, immensely opposed to acceptance of mankind's mediocrity, and fiercely belligerent against conservative compliance with what must be called the Establishment.

She proved her feelings as a Columbia student by giving up painting altogether. She refused to follow normal instruction practices, and left school. She abandoned the idea of an art career, and went back to her family in Virginia. Georgia at that moment relinquished art. Her emotions must have cut deeply. One cannot be an artist and toss art aside.

In the vacuum left, Georgia went with her sister to the University of Virginia summer school. Alon Bement, a professor of art from Columbia University, was in charge of Virginia's summer art program. Drawn by curiosity, Georgia visited his class. Something seemed different. She could not resist. She enrolled in the art class, and two weeks later Professor Bement asked her to teach in the school the next summer.[49]

Georgia thought that she was not qualified to teach. She did not have the experience. At that moment an offer came to her from Amarillo, Texas, asking her to supervise art instruction at their public schools. Why Georgia without teaching experience? Why Amarillo, a cattle town without paved roads? What could art mean down there? No matter; Georgia went.

This was truly the Wild West of her early dreams. It was a desert country, with few trees and too dry for flowers for her students to draw. It was windy and empty, in her own description. But it was Texas, and she stayed for four years, going on from Amarillo public schools to the West Texas Normal School— teaching prospective teachers. She loved the country, and she painted in exactly the way she wanted to paint, without Eastern inhibitions. Texas was free of inhibitions then, and maybe now it still is in some parts.

She wrote back to the friend in New York: "I got up at dawn to meet the morning train because it is so exciting to see it come through the sunrise." [49]

What did she mean, meeting a train? A black diesel engine box pulling a few second-hand passenger cars into an empty station? Times have changed. When Georgia O'Keeffe met that morning train, it was a locomotive with a bell and chuffing smoke, and a deep whistle that reverberated long and loud over the countryside. The chill morning air generated mists that hung low above the landscape, and the red sun just rising turned the world to a fiery glow. The small dark railroad station building would emerge slowly in sharp outline from the night's darkness, and from inside the station would come the inevitable clack-clacking of telegraph keys from a lighted office, the only indication of life anywhere until a man slowly shuffled into sight and pulled a creaky handtruck far down the gravel path to the point where the mail and baggage cars would stop.

Then, at last, to the one waiting, the roar of the train would roll over the prairies, a huge sweeping headlight to outshine the rising sun would grow larger and larger with the swift approach of the engine, and finally the train would pull up into a hissing and screeching stop at the station. Suddenly there would be people there, emerging from wagons and carriages to meet arrivals, people descending from steps with the help of porters, light pouring out from windows of another transitory world, shouting and noise. Then the engine bell would ring and with explosive chuffs of white smoke the train would slowly pick up momentum. Faster and faster it would go until it swept out of sight. Once more the lonely whistle would carry back, and the station fall into silence except for the eternal clack-clacking of the telegraph key from inside. The sun by then would be fully up in the sky.

This light, this color, this sound brought Georgia O'Keeffe, the young school teacher, to meet the train at dawn. If this imagined description is not exact, the essence of the feeling is there—of the morning train coming through the sunrise.

The image in that line she wrote to her friend in New York contained the soul of Georgia O'Keeffe herself. Her excitement in meeting a train goes far to explain why she had to become the artist which she has been. Keenly aware of the vibrancy of things, she translated what would seem commonplace to most people into her personal expression.

One day Georgia rolled up a group of her drawings, done in charcoal and pastel, and sent them off to her friend in New York. She had no purpose in sending them except to show Anita Pollitzer what she had been doing. In fact Georgia told Anita very clearly not to show them anywhere else.

Anita Pollitzer broke Georgia's injunction immediately. When she first unrolled the drawings in New York and looked at them, she realized that what Georgia O'Keeffe had done was something very different and special. She rolled them up again, and carried them straight to the owner of a small gallery on Fifth Avenue who was doing a great deal to help modern art and artists. His name was Alfred Stieglitz.

It was a rainy afternoon, Anita remembered. The elevator up to the gallery was out of order, and she had to walk up a steep flight of stairs carrying the roll of drawings under her arm. She found Stieglitz in his gallery, and she spread the drawings over the floor in front of him.

He looked down at them. Then he said, "Finally, a woman on paper."

To those drawings, done in charcoal on art students' sheets, Anita Pollitzer gave an even greater accolade. They said something, she remarked, that had not yet been said.[49]

Alfred Stieglitz decided at once, without ceremony, to give an exhibition of the drawings. The man who first introduced Rodin, Cézanne, Picasso and Matisse to the United States, was ready to introduce Georgia O'Keeffe, the unknown school teacher from the West. Who or what she was did not matter to Stieglitz. The drawings counted. "They ought to be given a chance," he said.[49]

Georgia O'Keeffe stayed in the West when her first exhibition in New York took place in Stieglitz's gallery at 291 Fifth Avenue. She did not really care. She did come the year after, when Stieglitz wished to give her a second show.

Then Georgia was swept into the fascinating New York world of Alfred Stieglitz.

THE little art gallery run by Stieglitz at 291 Fifth Avenue, New York, was never merely a business operation. It was a meeting place, a place for discussion, exchange of ideas. It was a place where new art and new painters hung on the walls, transferring to the visitor an excitement of discovery. People returned again and again, drawn to it, so that the gallery became like the *salon* of old. In the years before World War I the United States, and indeed the countries of Europe, were emerging from the Victorian era into the first pangs of the twentieth century. Change was evident everywhere. Alfred Stieglitz perhaps saw the future more clearly than most people. He used his gallery as an expression for his hopes for that future.

For those who did frequent the gallery—a strange assortment of all kinds of people—"291" became a kind of symbol of a way of life.[45]

It is true that Alfred Stieglitz brought the new Post-Impressionist art of Paris to America: the early Cubism of Picasso, the sheer design and drawing of Matisse, the shocking extremism of the French moderns from 1908 on. The Armory Show in New York did not occur until 1913. To Stieglitz, then, goes the earliest perception and anticipation of what was going to hit our country like a bombshell. The regular visitors to "291" apparently were not repelled by the "wild" European art. The genius that could open new views into an unknown, exciting future brought his friends back always to see more.

"291"

149

The genius was Stieglitz. His personality, his ideas, the far-reaching range of his influence for Americans perhaps meant more in the long run than even his early importation of French art. An outstanding description of Stieglitz at that time was written by Hutchins Hapgood, then a *New York Globe* newspaper writer. He described Stieglitz as a strenuous, never-sleeping spirit, something always alive. He called him a smoldering volcano, in whom the fire never died out and seldom subsided.[45]

Alfred Stieglitz must have had very definite ideas on almost everything. His thoughts were not cohesive enough to become in themselves a "philosophy." Rather through his conversation he stripped away false conceptions, smugness, unawareness about many things. He had the facility to make his listeners see differently than they had before. He touched the hidden nerves of life's values. Hapgood tells of the kinds of people who went regularly to "291" to hear Stieglitz talk as he moved among his paintings. Rich, poor, conventional, Bohemian, contented or unhappy, his audience was a slice through the stratas of society. Most of them had ready-made conventional beliefs. Stieglitz, continually talking, seldom listening, tore them down. Hapgood, who was one who could not stay away from the invigoration of "291" for more than a few weeks or months at the most, said that those who went a second time were not so sure of the "conventions" in art and life; those who returned again and again became less and less sure, more and more restless, possibly more and more unhappy, but more alive, more sensitive to reality.[45]

Into this world of Stieglitz, Georgia O'Keeffe dropped on her return to New York in 1917, when she was given a second exhibition at "291." This time the show was larger and more complete than the original one of drawings.

Georgia O'Keeffe's work through these and following years was in the almost purely abstract manner which she had developed while in Texas. She completely renounced the styles of her student and commercial art days. To find herself, she had to discover the barest and most basic elements in design. It would never have been her way to paint in abstraction only because other painters were doing so. French art was beginning to cross the Atlantic in waves, turning later to a flood. The Armory Show of 1913 in New York changed the American pattern of cultural thinking toward abstract art, and the distorted and broken elements of form as in Cubism.

Georgia O'Keeffe followed no one, but used abstract expression as a means of arriving at the basic elements of what she wanted to say. She stripped away everything, and then built again for herself slowly and over a period of time.

Her approach to art equaled in temperament Alfred Stieglitz's attitudes toward life. Stieglitz in his little gallery shone like a beacon to those who came to hear him talk, drawn irresistibly as moths. Suddenly at "291" there were two matching spirits. Both Stieglitz and O'Keeffe were fiercely individual. They were drawn to each other as two powerful magnets would be attracted.

Stieglitz was photographer as well as gallery owner and art dealer. His gallery seemed to grow out of his photography, and his showing of unknown art and artists in turn grew out of the gallery. Again in turn it was the art he showed which drew people the first time to his gallery and it was the force of his personality that influenced them to come back.

But photography was the base. Stieglitz was one of the first photographers to make an art out of a camera's use. To call him one of the first may be an underestimate. His photographs done at a time when knowledge of film was about equivalent to the production of the model T Ford, stand up today with the best of the highly skilled photographers using jet age equipment.

Yet even up to this moment an argument can rage between those who believe that photography—in single shots—is an art form, and those who consider it as a mechanical rendering of a subject. However skillfully done, state the latter, a cameraman is giving no more than a reproduction of the subject, an illustrated record, or a commercially slanted piece of propaganda. Adherents of photography can point to remarkable compositions of subject, of color work done in the abstract, of pictures made from nature or live models that express the personality of the man behind the lens as much as any painting proves the artist.

When viewing the results by Stieglitz, the arguments about photography seem in retrospect to fall silent, or become void. His pictures live in themselves, whether as fine art or as reproduction. What he did was simply his own. His personal use of a camera became so distinctly individual that nothing mattered except that Stieglitz did it. In this area of thinking, he was indeed a forerunner of the line of great photographers who snap not just for newsworthy or art-like similarities but who have endeavored to use the camera as a means of its own.

After Georgia O'Keeffe entered the circle of friends who surrounded Alfred Stieglitz, she literally "came" into the picture, too. She was his model for a long series of portrait photographs over a period of time. His strong personality seems even to affect the camera itself. He would have had to be strong just to catch her own individuality and strength.

A story is told of a young woman who gazed at Stieglitz's photographs of Georgia for a long time, and then began to cry. When asked about the tears, all she could say was, "He loves her so!" [45] *

He did love her, and in 1924 they were married. It was union of two geniuses. Both reached into the rare atmosphere of accomplishment, Stieglitz with new horizons in photography and Georgia with an outpouring of paintings. She did paintings of New York with an eye that saw the city in a different way than anyone else has seen it. She moved into flower painting which initially brought her such popularity and fame. She was free to paint exactly as she pleased and she did, carrying all before her with her absolute originality of style.

From the year 1923 until 1946 Georgia O'Keeffe had a one-man exhibition in New York every year at Stieglitz's gallery. This meant a prodigious amount of painting. New York was her headquarters through these years, but she traveled, too; Lake George where Stieglitz and Georgia spent summers for a time; to Nova Scotia and islands in the south, but especially to New Mexico. She visited the Far West again, and found New Mexico and its high mountains and arid deserts, in 1929. She was forty-two. Immediately her paintings reflected new horizons, great new discoveries.

THE
STIEGLITZ
ERA

ALFRED STIEGLITZ was the man who "discovered" Georgia O'Keeffe. He showed her drawings to the public for the first time, and introduced her to the art world. He discovered other artists,

---

* Note: the picture of Georgia O'Keeffe (Plate 22) is an original charcoal pencil drawing by Winthrop Neilson, done after a study of Alfred Stieglitz's photographs and particularly after seeing a reproduction of one taken by him in 1918 in the book "Victorian in the Modern World" by Hutchins Hapgood (Harcourt, Brace & Co., 1939). The latter photograph shows Miss O'Keeffe's strong, intense personality. Other reproduced photographs of the same time indicate a softer, almost mischievous side. Because none of these photographs were found for reproduction here, the co-author has executed his own interpretation of a very great artist.

too—not only the Frenchmen already recognized abroad whose work he brought to America, but American painters and photographers who needed recognition. It is worth pausing for a moment to think of the impact of the "Stieglitz era."

The expression "to discover" an artist is trite, inadequate, and bears little reference to what actually happens. Usually a professional in the arts must try in many ways to gain recognition. But suppose that Georgia O'Keeffe's friend had given in to her demand that no one else see the drawings she sent from Texas? Or suppose the bad weather had discouraged Anita Pollitzer from going down to the "291" Gallery that day? Would the story of Georgia O'Keeffe have been different, and would she have been able to be included in this book of great women painters of all time?

Undoubtedly she would have, because her vitality and skill in painting would have shown itself through another outlet. "Talent" or "genius," in those words which do not mean any longer what they were intended to mean, usually comes out. All the same, it is possible that Georgia O'Keeffe might have remained a local artist in Texas, teaching high school teachers.

Not long ago a girl graduating from an art school was selected, without applying and without her previous knowledge, by an Eastern university to fill out a special group in a post-graduate program. It was indeed an honor earned completely unexpectedly through her own potential possibilities as shown in her undergraduate work.

Earlier in the book, the suggestion was made that artists must have not only technical qualifications and skill, plus a truly creative intelligence, but should have also what can be called "luck," or the happy circumstances of being in the right place at the right time. How does one make this possible? One cannot, of course. Yet keen perception tries to anticipate the chance, and how it might happen.

Georgia O'Keeffe, who went through art instruction and then a commercial job before renouncing them altogether, felt every emotion that the artist must stand. She realized finally as every artist must, that the urge toward art cannot be denied by those who live for it alone. Georgia was "lucky." She found Stieglitz. Or Stieglitz found her.

Alfred Stieglitz, born in 1864 during the Civil War, brought into light other painters beside his wife, Georgia O'Keeffe. Primarily, as said before, he was a photographer. He found quickly enough that art galleries would not accept photographs as art. To show his own pictures, and the camera pictures of other photographers, he was pushed into opening his own gallery for that purpose—the famous "291." Along with photography, he included paintings on his walls.

Max Weber, Arthur Dove, and Marsden Hartley were among the American group who achieved fame through Stieglitz. These artists who made their names at that time helped to form that glittering circle of Stieglitz's group who lived around his gallery.[48]

Another name is John Marin. No one regarded his own wife more highly than Stieglitz did. Yet even Stieglitz yielded first place to Marin over Georgia.

John Marin has been thought by many to be the greatest artist to live and paint in the United States. Others may say Thomas Eakins, or Winslow Homer, or in this present day Andrew Wyeth. Why John Marin? He is known best for watercolors and drawings, although he did some outstanding oil paintings, too. John Marin can make his own statement, as put down in his handwriting in a numbered portfolio in the authors' possession:

"There must be an order—there is an order. From the years of seeings and observings the swirl of movements obey the laws of motion. People do not—unless in panic—run helter skelter on streets. Too, buildings obey their laws of construction. Granted: but there creeps in another set of laws, a seeming wayward set of laws, the law of the Spirit and the law of life. The law of the seeings which grips the sensitive, grips him in all its being—he with the traveling eye, he with the eye that takes in, step by step. Then, of a verity, buildings, streets, people, become a solid mass of moving aliveness. Nothing is dead, with a kind of order to it all, played on a few key strings . . .

"That is the eternal job of the artist, in all forms, his symbol everlasting to make a complete living organ, which lives of its own right, gotten by his rebounds."[51]

Marin sought out the living essentials of things, whether they were so simple as a sailboat on the sea, or a cluster of cherry trees in blossom on a hill. His feelings of the essential were the same as Georgia O'Keeffe's, and the same, expressed individually, of every one of the artists whom Stieglitz sponsored through his gallery shows. All together became a group, a Stieglitz circle in a way, bound by the eternal effort to get down to the roots of nature and life. The consensus of their ideas pulled them close by a term never used: the Stieglitz concordance of spirit. Alfred Stieglitz wrote of himself, "I was born in Hoboken. I am an American. Photography is my passion. The search for truth is my obsession." [9]

In 1946, the last year of Georgia O'Keeffe's regular annual one-man exhibitions, two events happened, one a crowning joy, the other a tragic blow. The first was a major retrospective show of her lifetime work put on by the Museum of Modern Art in New York—an occasion which would cap the career of any artist. Georgia O'Keeffe achieved then the laurels of her greatness.

In that same year during the summer, she lost Alfred Stieglitz. He died in his 82nd year, world-renowned for his photography and honored for his service to art in America. He died loved by his admirers and followers, writers, artists, friends who knew him so well, the public, and the painters who had achieved recognition through him. Of the latter, one was his own wife, Georgia O'Keeffe.[48] He used to say, when she had done a painting, "That is Georgia!" [49]

For the next three years Georgia O'Keeffe gave all of her time to sorting and identifying the paintings in Stieglitz's collection, the photographs he had taken, and the papers in his files. The collection, including sculpture and the photographs, were divided carefully and presented to art centers over the country. So she carried out her husband's wish that all the results of his life's work should be given to the public.

With the task completed, Georgia O'Keeffe returned to New Mexico and resumed her painting. Once again she worked tirelessly, producing enough for a new show in New York in 1950. Exhibition after exhibition have followed—in New York, Worcester, New Mexico—and her work is part of museum collections all across the country.

She continues her painting—she sent one to the Whitney Museum Annual 1968—and there are few who know anything of art who do not appreciate Georgia O'Keeffe. All who know her work wait expectantly for the new paintings which must continue to come from her brush in New Mexico.

NOT LONG AGO Dr. Evan Turner, Director of the Philadelphia Museum of Art, talked to a group of art students and said, in effect, that in certain ways traditions of art changed and changed back again. He made the point that from the era of the Renaissance the remembered artists were those well-known in their lifetimes: i.e., Raphael, Leonardo, Michelangelo and others of lesser stature. Later, as Dr. Turner explained, in the first years of the 19th century after the French Revolution, the patronage patterns changed, and the reverse was true, that many of the most distinguished artists of the next one hundred years were generally only appreciated in the later time of their lives, or even, in a few outstanding cases, after their deaths. From this situation stems the old truism that only after he is dead does an artist's painting become valuable.

But times may have changed once again today. Dr. Turner stated that perhaps now, with the unbridled passion of a new generation of often inexperienced collectors, there is such a wild scramble for the unknown artist that it is hard to believe that potentially distinguished artists are not known in their own lifetimes, although, admittedly, they may not be fully appreciated.

Perhaps Dr. Turner's point is debatable. Who can know? The course of art changes so rapidly now that yesterday's gallery fashion is tomorrow's forgotten man. The competition today among artists is intense. It seems that desire to make a reputation and the urge to survive in the marketplace becomes to many artists more important than the expression of sincere work.

Sincere artists have traditionally hoped that their work would "live," permanently. It has been a code, for example, to use pigments and materials in painting that would last. Dr. Turner, however, expressed a feeling that at this time many artists are not concerned about permanence, that they are only interested in the present without consideration for the future. This is a radically different concept.

Is this attitude so questionable after all? How about writers who produce books—factual or fiction—which they know will not "live" for more than a few current months? Most theatre and film productions are not expected to endure for posterity; they are not created for that intention.

The art students who heard Dr. Turner must make up their own minds on this very provocative point. The painters of times past went so far as to mix their own colors with great care for permanency. Of course, no art stores existed around the corner to furnish paints made up by unknown chemists. They had to trust themselves. Few painters take this trouble now. The art store is too convenient. In a transitory life, with the hydrogen bomb aimed night and day at everything he does, should an artist take the future seriously?

Current doubters should note the record of Georgia O'Keeffe, a painter who has been working consistently for some sixty years. It is certain that through her life she has never asked herself the questions that plague some younger artists. She merely has done what she wanted to do from those first moments when she knew. From there she has let her own individual will express itself. She is a great contemporary example of one who has never wavered in faith or loyalty to her profession.

A record of so many successful years will not be easily erased. Georgia O'Keeffe has, in her lifetime, established such a firm reputation that no future changes in taste can weaken it. She did not plan it so, she simply did it.

Of all women painters, Georgia O'Keeffe has probably done the most to shatter the myth that women cannot be artists. As one looks at the great outpouring of her work now so widely distributed and respected, should one think that this production of art was created by a woman rather than a man? Or that it makes a difference?

The surprising answer is that it does make a difference. Georgia O'Keeffe's art is basically that of a woman.

Not that her painting is in any way "feminine." It is strong and rugged with New Mexican hills and mountains and bones in the desert. A man might equally have done these. But in the delicacy of her vivid flower compositions appearing almost abstract in some cases, she has achieved results so individual that no woman or man has ever come close to them. It is doubtful if a man could. To accomplish them needed the perception of a woman.

Georgia O'Keeffe's career really began with the abstract drawings which Stieglitz showed in 1916. She maintained an abstract or semi-abstract feeling through much of her work, even though at first glance the paintings appear sharply realistic. She used walls with doorways, but which went further in composition to a "super-realism," something more important than the subject itself. They preceded the non-realistic squares and rectangles which characterize many younger, more contemporary artists. The same is true of the stark barns, houses, and churches which O'Keeffe painted.

The impact of her art comes not from what she included of

157

realistic nature in her paintings, but what she left *out*. Nothing remains of realism except what is necessary to express the depth and substance of feeling. This is as good a definition as anything of "super-realism," or the use of nature to produce a work of art that imparts only the essence of the subject.

To leave out of a picture the non-essentials and include only the essentials is not new in art. It is typical of the primitives, the Early Christians, and all down through the ages including El Greco to the recent "minimal" artists who reduce their conceptions to the point of practically nothing. In a far different way than Georgia O'Keeffe, Andrew Wyeth is a "super-realist," not a realist or naturalist at all, as is commonly supposed. He achieves his spectacular success by what he leaves out of his paintings, keeping only the essentials which he remembers of the subject. Aside from portraits, Wyeth does most of his paintings in his studio from memory, after having spent long hours studying his subject on the spot.

To know what to leave out is one of the ultimate and perhaps final tests for the artist. If a painting must communicate something to the viewer, the communication comes through its virtually indescribable aura, or feeling—its "essence."

The quality of Georgia O'Keeffe has been to understand this. She understood it so well that she almost gave up painting altogether as a young girl in disgust at the conventions which she was being taught. Then she gained the skill of capturing the basic quality of things, and she never again wavered. This skill kept her flowers from becoming sentimental, her bones from being mawkish.

All through her lifetime she has remained consistent in her outlook. In moving from the abstract into the compositions taken from nature she changed subjects depending on where she was. She often did series of paintings with the same theme. One was a number of crosses, first started in Nova Scotia where commemorative crosses stand on hills overlooking a black sea. She did more of these in the Southwest. Then the bones have been a prevailing theme for a long period.

Georgia O'Keeffe is probably most familiar to the public, not only for the bones, but also for her flower compositions. She could turn one rose into a canvas of seemingly limitless size. She would take a single petal and the throat of a morning glory and make the viewer feel the impact of life by gazing down into the mysteries of the flower. The paintings glowed with color, jewel-like in conception.

One more point about Georgia O'Keeffe should be remembered. In her life and her work she has been utterly American. It is not likely that any European could discover the breadth and grandeur of nature, as well as its minute qualities, in the way she has. Her strong spirit, her contempt for the trivial, her independence, and her unceasing work have all made of her an artist whom Americans can call uniquely their own.

In days when conformity is expected of everyone, Georgia O'Keeffe has never conformed. She is an individual. No wonder she lives among the great spaces of the Southwest, where the winds blow fresh. There, against the magnitude of nature where even the morning train coming out of the sunrise creeps over the desert like a small speck, O'Keeffe has always found herself.

THE early paintings of Georgia O'Keeffe were abstract. She needed abstraction as a sort of "shedding" of naturalistic reproduction in order to find an elemental basis in the meaning of art. She had to get rid of the superficial, the idea that a painting must only represent "something recognizable and familiar."

In her case, painting in abstract style was not meant to be an end in itself. The European painters were creating art less and less representational, more into abstract realms as a new road moving into unknown areas. They never expected to return. O'Keeffe, on the other hand, simply used abstract painting as a tool to clear her mind. Then she went on with forms understandable as walls, flowers, bones, mountains.

Hers was an unusual approach. Ordinarily artists seek to find their own style as a *way* of saying what they want to say. They maintain and develop that style, or they revise it, or they drop it altogether for a different style which they think will state their intentions better. The *way* in which they paint is of primary concern. This is normal, and the way it usually should be.

If one can interpret Georgia O'Keeffe's intentions correctly, she used the first non-realistic painting not to say something, but to find out *what* to say. Once she did find what she wanted to communicate, she made the discovery that it could be expressed either in abstract terms or more realistically or recognizably. For her, it really did not matter what style of painting was used. The substance of her communication was there anyway.

Not many painters could do what she did. Non-objective or objective, her work leads into the same inner secret places of nature. Georgia O'Keeffe found her own world and each painting does not matter at all. The same world is beyond.

So, although she did begin with abstraction, and then used semi-realism followed by stark realism, Georgia O'Keeffe has never really changed at all. Everything she has done, from high-keyed abstract to gaunt tree trunks, is not only consistent, but consistently O'Keeffe.

A drawing called simply "Abstraction" (Plate 23) is a highly provocative use of forms. The dramatic lines crossing diagonally in a fast downward push are countered by the great globe form behind, which itself is abruptly pulled in on the left hand side. Of course, the group of six black dashes in space hold the drawing, and attention.

The composition of this drawing is so subtle as to defy brief analysis. The converging black lines are filled with tremendous *downward* force, not upward due to the angle in the smaller line just above the arc. The great globe is immeasurable in size. The small lines, seemingly so casually placed but actually done with great thought in size and spacing, are moving at high speed, downward they appear although at first glance they could have been going outward. These lines control in the drawing the pressure of the push of the strong diagonals.

Let no one read into an abstract work literal meanings. There is a tendency of many people—the literal-minded ones—to do this, even today after years of exposure to non-realistic art. A purely abstract piece of art is to be taken for what it is—an expression divorced not from reality, for there is the reality of feelings, of senses and ideas, but divorced from the reality of things themselves.

Georgia O'Keeffe meant her drawing to be interpreted this way, as a reality of forces felt with the mind, not something objectively seen with the eye.

There is her painting with a literal title, "Wave, Night" (Color Plate 7). The soft white transverse line is unmistakably a wave, although literal waves are seldom that straight. The wash of a preceding wave on a beach, and the dim horizon line are apparent. What of the barely perceivable lines arching toward the horizon? And what is that one fantastic dot of white on the horizon? A boat at sea? It is very doubtful if Miss O'Keeffe intended that. It is something within herself.

"Peach and Glass" is a simply conceived painting, almost an exercise in composition. It is interesting as an unusual subject for her, known as she is for her other things. But it is Georgia O'Keeffe, always consistent in feeling and quality of nature.

The world knows her best for her many paintings of bones, and the hills and deserts of her beloved New Mexico. "Red Hills and Bones" (Color Plate 8) is one. This painting is remarkable in a number of ways. It is strong, powerful, limitless. The loneliness, desolation, and stark beauty of the land pull the viewer into the canvas itself. From the immediacy of the bleached bones in the foreground to the massive bleak red hill and the fantastic mountain shapes behind it, the painting hits with haunting force.

Technically, it is interesting to examine the skill of the drawing of the bone forms. The leg and spinal vertebrae, bleached white long ago by the sun, are done with care. Yet the drawing is never so overdone as to distract the eye from the mountain beyond. The bones are a part of the whole.

The space between the foreground and the great red hill cannot be measured. It is vast. The hill itself takes form and solidity through the subtle use of light and shadows. A streak of sunlight indicates the concave form. The shading to the right establishes the roundness and bulk of the huge hill. An unseen cloud casts shadows across the top. The deep furrows down the dry barren sides of the slope complement the hard, dry bones and, indeed, take on similar shapes with the vertebrae.

One of the most interesting aspects of the whole painting is that the colors of the far mountain shapes in the background are actually stronger than the red color of the hill. In lesser hands, the balancing of the painting would be thrown off, and the further mountains would appear nearer than the hill. Georgia O'Keeffe used the massiveness through shading of the red hill to push the further mountains back where they belong. Much of the painting's vitality comes from this constant pressure of distant planes against each other. Dead and dry as the subject seems, it is alive with its opposing forces.

Space, immensity, grandeur, bleakness and forces of nature combine to make a masterpiece. The elements of the earlier abstract drawing are brought to fulfillment here.

Georgia O'Keeffe, great American painter, interprets America itself through vision and perception as wide and mighty as the mountains she paints.

164

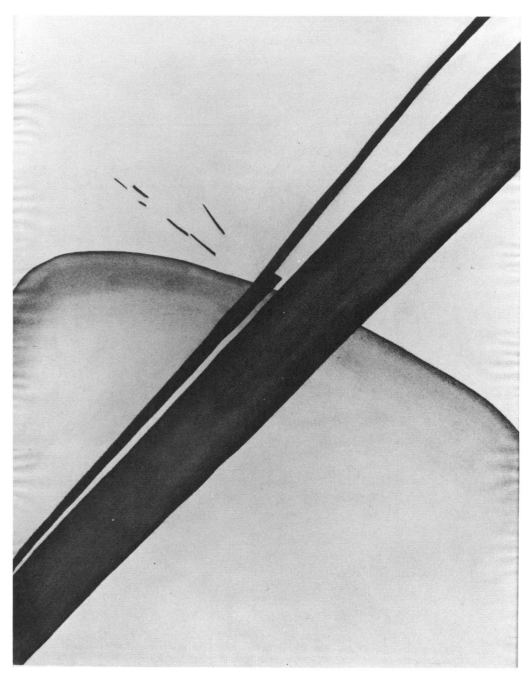

PLATE 23

Abstraction, by Georgia O'Keeffe.
*Addison Gallery of American Art,
Phillips Academy, Andover.*

Here is a work that expresses only a mood, as the abstract drawing did. It is a painting caught from nature, but there is nothing literal in it. It must be "seen" with the mind.

This outstanding painting of Georgia O'Keeffe's gives one a feeling of the deep mystery of night across the sea toward a spot of strange light through enveloping darkness. It is a quiet painting, and yet contains all the restless motion of the ocean. To anyone who has stood long on the night seashore and understood the near presence of the entire universe pressing close, "Wave, Night" will awaken a response. The response, though, cannot help but be abstract, a response felt with the emotions, not by logical or practical explanation.

The longer one looks at this painting, the more keenly perceived is the immensity of space, the quietness, the mystery.

So where, then, is the difference between "Abstraction" and "Wave, Night"? In way of communication, they are intrinsically the same. This is what Georgia O'Keeffe learned by moving from pure abstract to use of nature. The means of expressing substance can be universal.

How, then, does one interpret the little still life, "Peach and Glass" (Plate 24)? Three prosaic objects on a table do not lend themselves to abstractions of forces and glory of the night sea. The fruit, the plate and the glass are perfectly recognizable.

The painting here has abandoned abstraction, but the same simplicity and essentials are expressed. The three objects are used for a still life which communicates the principles of substance. More plainly, the peach is more than a piece of fruit. The glass, too common an article to convey any drama or feeling, establishes itself as *this* glass, not just any glass. The plate becomes *the* plate, not *a* plate. Georgia O'Keeffe used the quality of the absolute in many of her paintings of windows or doorways set in plain walls, in her flowers, her series of shrines with crosses.

Painters have always used fruit, glasses, bottles for still life pictures. Few have touched the ultimate actuality of their subject so completely. It is an elusive quality in which O'Keeffe excels.

Typical of her, too, is the use of only one peach on the plate, and one glass. Three objects and a section of table take up the whole picture space. She often did this with her flowers: one bloom, even several petals alone fill her canvas. Her composition of the objects proves again her knowledge and intuition. Practical accuracy of perspective yields to necessities of planning the relationship of forms.

PLATE 24

Peach and Glass, 1927, by Georgia O'Keeffe.
Collection of Philadelphia Museum of Art.

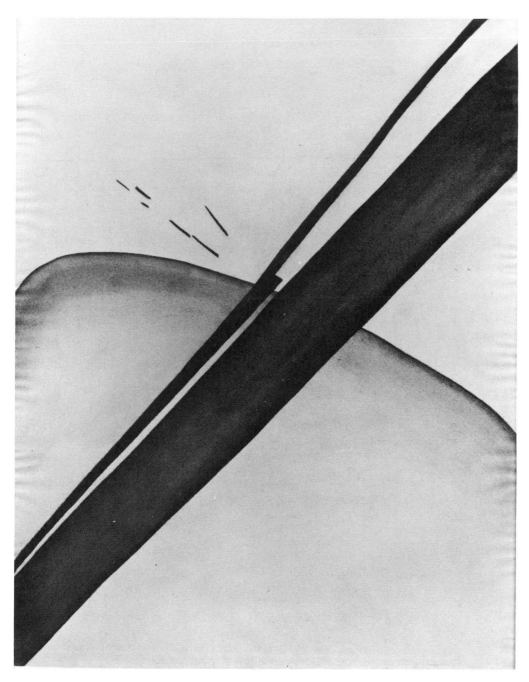

PLATE 23

Abstraction, by Georgia O'Keeffe.
Addison Gallery of American Art,
Phillips Academy, Andover.

Here is a work that expresses only a mood, as the abstract drawing did. It is a painting caught from nature, but there is nothing literal in it. It must be "seen" with the mind.

This outstanding painting of Georgia O'Keeffe's gives one a feeling of the deep mystery of night across the sea toward a spot of strange light through enveloping darkness. It is a quiet painting, and yet contains all the restless motion of the ocean. To anyone who has stood long on the night seashore and understood the near presence of the entire universe pressing close, "Wave, Night" will awaken a response. The response, though, cannot help but be abstract, a response felt with the emotions, not by logical or practical explanation.

The longer one looks at this painting, the more keenly perceived is the immensity of space, the quietness, the mystery.

So where, then, is the difference between "Abstraction" and "Wave, Night"? In way of communication, they are intrinsically the same. This is what Georgia O'Keeffe learned by moving from pure abstract to use of nature. The means of expressing substance can be universal.

How, then, does one interpret the little still life, "Peach and Glass" (Plate 24)? Three prosaic objects on a table do not lend themselves to abstractions of forces and glory of the night sea. The fruit, the plate and the glass are perfectly recognizable.

The painting here has abandoned abstraction, but the same simplicity and essentials are expressed. The three objects are used for a still life which communicates the principles of substance. More plainly, the peach is more than a piece of fruit. The glass, too common an article to convey any drama or feeling, establishes itself as *this* glass, not just any glass. The plate becomes *the* plate, not *a* plate. Georgia O'Keeffe used the quality of the absolute in many of her paintings of windows or doorways set in plain walls, in her flowers, her series of shrines with crosses.

Painters have always used fruit, glasses, bottles for still life pictures. Few have touched the ultimate actuality of their subject so completely. It is an elusive quality in which O'Keeffe excels.

Typical of her, too, is the use of only one peach on the plate, and one glass. Three objects and a section of table take up the whole picture space. She often did this with her flowers: one bloom, even several petals alone fill her canvas. Her composition of the objects proves again her knowledge and intuition. Practical accuracy of perspective yields to necessities of planning the relationship of forms.

Peach and Glass, 1927, by Georgia O'Keeffe.
Collection of Philadelphia Museum of Art.

"Peach and Glass" is a simply conceived painting, almost an exercise in composition. It is interesting as an unusual subject for her, known as she is for her other things. But it is Georgia O'Keeffe, always consistent in feeling and quality of nature.

The world knows her best for her many paintings of bones, and the hills and deserts of her beloved New Mexico. "Red Hills and Bones" (Color Plate 8) is one. This painting is remarkable in a number of ways. It is strong, powerful, limitless. The loneliness, desolation, and stark beauty of the land pull the viewer into the canvas itself. From the immediacy of the bleached bones in the foreground to the massive bleak red hill and the fantastic mountain shapes behind it, the painting hits with haunting force.

Technically, it is interesting to examine the skill of the drawing of the bone forms. The leg and spinal vertebrae, bleached white long ago by the sun, are done with care. Yet the drawing is never so overdone as to distract the eye from the mountain beyond. The bones are a part of the whole.

The space between the foreground and the great red hill cannot be measured. It is vast. The hill itself takes form and solidity through the subtle use of light and shadows. A streak of sunlight indicates the concave form. The shading to the right establishes the roundness and bulk of the huge hill. An unseen cloud casts shadows across the top. The deep furrows down the dry barren sides of the slope complement the hard, dry bones and, indeed, take on similar shapes with the vertebrae.

One of the most interesting aspects of the whole painting is that the colors of the far mountain shapes in the background are actually stronger than the red color of the hill. In lesser hands, the balancing of the painting would be thrown off, and the further mountains would appear nearer than the hill. Georgia O'Keeffe used the massiveness through shading of the red hill to push the further mountains back where they belong. Much of the painting's vitality comes from this constant pressure of distant planes against each other. Dead and dry as the subject seems, it is alive with its opposing forces.

Space, immensity, grandeur, bleakness and forces of nature combine to make a masterpiece. The elements of the earlier abstract drawing are brought to fulfillment here.

Georgia O'Keeffe, great American painter, interprets America itself through vision and perception as wide and mighty as the mountains she paints.